JAMESTOWN  EDUCATION

W9-CJN-379

TIMED READINGS

Third Edition

Fifty 400-Word Passages
with Questions for
Building Reading Speed

BOOK SEVEN

Edward Spargo

 **Glencoe McGraw-Hill**

New York, New York   Columbus, Ohio   Chicago, Illinois   Peoria, Illinois   Woodland Hills, California

JAMESTOWN EDUCATION

Titles in This Series
Timed Readings, Third Edition
Timed Readings in Literature

Teaching Notes are available for this text and
will be sent to the instructor. Please write on
school stationery; tell us what grade
you teach and identify the text.

Glencoe/McGraw-Hill
*A Division of The **McGraw·Hill** Companies*

Timed Readings, Third Edition
Book Seven

Cover and text design: Deborah Hulsey Christie

ISBN: 0-89061-509-8

Send all queries:
Glencoe/McGraw-Hill
8787 Orion Place
Columbus, OH 43240-4027

14 15 16 021 10 09 08 07

Contents

Introduction to the Student

These *Timed Readings* are designed to help you become a faster and better reader. As you progress through the book, you will find yourself growing in reading speed and comprehension. You will be challenged to increase your reading rate while maintaining a high level of comprehension.

Reading, like most things, improves with practice. If you practice improving your reading speed, you will improve. As you will see, the rewards of improved reading speed will be well worth your time and effort.

Why Read Faster?

The quick and simple answer is that faster readers are better readers. Does this statement surprise you? You might think that fast readers would miss something and their comprehension might suffer. This is not true, for two reasons:

1. **Faster readers comprehend faster.** When you read faster, the writer's message is coming to you faster and makes sense sooner. Ideas are interconnected. The writer's thoughts are all tied together, each one leading to the next. The more quickly you can see how ideas are related to each other, the more quickly you can comprehend the meaning of what you are reading.

2. **Faster readers concentrate better.** Concentration is essential for comprehension. If your mind is wandering you can't understand what you are reading. A lack of concentration causes you to re-read, sometimes over and over, in order to comprehend. Faster readers concentrate better because there's less time for distractions to interfere. Comprehension, in turn, contributes to concentration. If you are concentrating and comprehending, you will not become distracted.

Want to Read More?

Do you wish that you could read more? (or, at least, would you like to do your required reading in less time?) Faster reading will help.

The illustration on the next page shows the number of books someone might read over a period of ten years. Let's see what faster reading could do for you. Look at the stack of books read by a slow reader and the stack

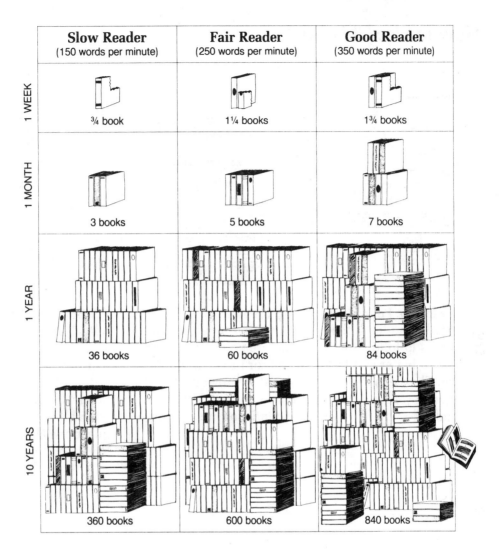

	Slow Reader (150 words per minute)	Fair Reader (250 words per minute)	Good Reader (350 words per minute)
1 WEEK	¾ book	1¼ books	1¾ books
1 MONTH	3 books	5 books	7 books
1 YEAR	36 books	60 books	84 books
10 YEARS	360 books	600 books	840 books

read by a good reader. (We show a speed of 350 words a minute for our "good" reader, but many fast readers can more than double that speed.) Let's say, however, that you are now reading at a rate of 150 words a minute. The illustration shows you reading 36 books a year. By increasing your reading speed to 250 words a minute, you could increase the number of books to 60 a year.

We have arrived at these numbers by assuming that the readers in our illustration read for one hour a day, six days a week, and that an average book is about 72,000 words long. Many people do not read that much, but they might if they could learn to read better and faster.

Faster reading doesn't *take* time, it *saves* time!

How to Use This Book

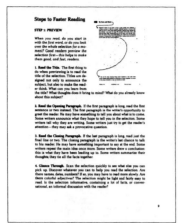

1 Learn the Four Steps
Study and learn the four steps to follow to become a better and faster reader. The steps are covered on pages 9, 10, 11, and 12.

2 Preview
Turn to the selection you are going to read and wait for the instructor's signal to preview. Your instructor will allow 30 seconds for previewing.

3 Begin reading
When your instructor gives you the signal, begin reading. Read at a slightly faster-than-normal speed. Read well enough so that you will be able to answer questions about what you have read.

7 Fill in the progress graph
Enter your score and plot your reading time on the graph on page 118 or 119. The right-hand side of the graph shows your words-per-minute reading speed. Write this number at the bottom of the page on the line labeled *Words per Minute.*

4 Record your time

When you finish reading, look at the blackboard and note your reading time. Your reading time will be the lowest time remaining on the board, or the next number to be erased. Write this time at the bottom of the page on the line labeled *Reading Time*.

5 Answer the questions

Answer the ten questions on the next page. There are five fact questions and five thought questions. Pick the *best* answer to each question and put an x in the box beside it.

6 Correct your answers

Using the Answer Key on pages 116 and 117, correct your work. Circle your wrong answers and put an x in the box you should have marked. Score 10 points for each correct answer. Write your score at the bottom of the page on the line labeled *Comprehension Score*.

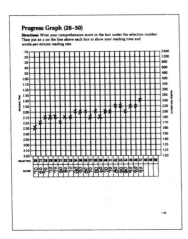

Instructions for the Pacing Drills

From time to time your instructor may wish to conduct pacing drills using *Timed Readings.* For this work you need to use the Pacing Dots printed in the margins of your book pages. The dots will help you regulate your reading speed to match the pace set by your instructor or announced on the reading cassette tape.

◄ Pacing Dots

You will be reading at the correct pace if you are at the dot when your instructor says "Mark" or when you hear a tone on the tape. If you are ahead of the pace, read a little more slowly; if you are behind the pace, increase your reading speed. Try to match the pace exactly.

Follow these steps.

Step 1: Record the pace. At the bottom of the page, write on the line labeled *Words per Minute* the rate announced by the instructor or by the speaker on the tape.

Step 2: Begin reading. Wait for the signal to begin reading. Read at a slightly faster-than-normal speed. You will not know how on-target your pace is until you hear your instructor say "Mark" or until you hear the first tone on the tape. After a little practice you will be able to select an appropriate starting speed most of the time.

Step 3: Adjust your pace. As you read, try to match the pace set by the instructor or the tape. Read more slowly or more quickly as necessary. You should be reading the line beside the dot when you hear the pacing signal. The pacing sounds may distract you at first. Don't worry about it. Keep reading and your concentration will return.

Step 4: Stop and answer questions. Stop reading when you are told to, even if you have not finished the selection. Answer the questions right away. Correct your work and record your score on the line *Comprehension Score.* Strive to maintain 80 percent comprehension on each drill as you gradually increase your pace.

Step 5: Fill in the pacing graph. Transfer your words-per-minute rate to the box labeled *Pace* on the pacing graph on page 120. Then plot your comprehension score on the line above the box.

These pacing drills are designed to help you become a more flexible reader. They encourage you to "break out" of a pattern of reading everything at the same speed.

The drills help in other ways, too. Sometimes in a reading program you reach a certain level and bog down. You don't seem able to move on and progress. The pacing drills will help you to work your way out of such slumps and get your reading program moving again.

Steps to Faster Reading

STEP 1: PREVIEW

When you read, do you start in with the first word, or do you look over the whole selection for a moment? Good readers preview the selection first—this helps to make them good, and fast, readers.

1. Read the Title. The first thing to do when previewing is to read the title of the selection. Titles are designed not only to announce the subject, but also to make the reader think. What can you learn from the title? What thoughts does it bring to mind? What do you already know about this subject?

2. Read the Opening Paragraph. If the first paragraph is long, read the first sentence or two instead. The first paragraph is the writer's opportunity to greet the reader. He may have something to tell you about what is to come. Some writers announce what they hope to tell you in the selection. Some writers tell why they are writing. Some writers just try to get the reader's attention—they may ask a provocative question.

3. Read the Closing Paragraph. If the last paragraph is long, read just the final line or two. The closing paragraph is the writer's last chance to talk to his reader. He may have something important to say at the end. Some writers repeat the main idea once more. Some writers draw a conclusion: this is what they have been leading up to. Some writers summarize their thoughts; they tie all the facts together.

4. Glance Through. Scan the selection quickly to see what else you can pick up. Discover whatever you can to help you read the selection. Are there names, dates, numbers? If so, you may have to read more slowly. Are there colorful adjectives? The selection might be light and fairly easy to read. Is the selection informative, containing a lot of facts, or conversational, an informal discussion with the reader?

By Sun and Stars

Migratory birds do not travel as fast as some people once believed. A German scientist in 1895, for example, attributed speeds in excess of 200 miles an hour to some birds during migration. Research later showed that this estimate was much too high. The peregrine falcon flies 165 to 180 miles per hour while chasing food, but very few birds can fly this fast. Birds have two speeds. One is for normal flying, and a faster one is for escaping enemies or chasing food. Most songbirds have cruising speeds between 25 and 50 miles per hour during migration.

One of the most amazing things about migration is that some birds raised without adult guidance or experience in actual migration can orient to the proper direction across vast stretches of water.

Reading Time _____ Comprehension Score _____ Words per Minute _____ 57

flying normal towers stage migration. some cruising pelicans, time subtle scientists close

Steps to Faster Reading

STEP 2: READ FOR MEANING

When you read, do you just see words? Are you so occupied reading words that you sometimes fail to get the meaning? Good readers see beyond the words—they read for meaning. This makes them faster readers.

1. Build Concentration. You cannot read with understanding if you are not concentrating. Every reader's mind wanders occasionally; it is not a cause for alarm. When you discover that your thoughts have strayed, correct the situation right away. The longer you wait, the harder it becomes. Avoid distractions and distracting situations. Outside noises and activities will compete for your attention if you let them. Keep the preview information in mind as you read. This will help to focus your attention on the selection.

2. Read in Thought Groups. Individual words do not tell us much. They must be combined with other words in order to yield meaning. To obtain meaning from the printed page, therefore, the reader should see the words in meaningful combinations. If you see only a word at a time (called word-by-word reading), your comprehension suffers along with your speed. To improve both speed and comprehension, try to group the words into phrases which have a natural relationship to each other. For practice, you might want to read aloud, trying to speak the words in meaningful combinations.

3. Question the Author. To sustain the pace you have set for yourself, and to maintain a high level of comprehension, question the writer as you read. Continually ask yourself such questions as, "What does this mean? What is he saying now? How can I use this information?" Questions like these help you to concentrate fully on the selection.

Steps to Faster Reading

STEP 3: GRASP PARAGRAPH SENSE

The paragraph is the basic unit of meaning. If you can discover quickly and understand the main point of each paragraph, you can comprehend the author's message. Good readers know how to find the main ideas of paragraphs quickly. This helps to make them faster readers.

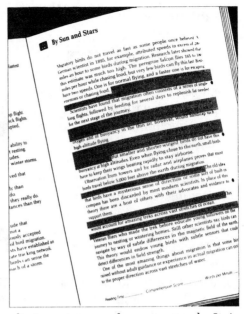

1. Find the Topic Sentence. The topic sentence, the sentence containing the main idea, is often the first sentence of a paragraph. It is followed by other sentences which support, develop, or explain the main idea. Sometimes a topic sentence comes at the end of a paragraph. When it does, the supporting details come first, building the base for the topic sentence. Some paragraphs do not have a topic sentence. Such paragraphs usually create a mood or feeling, rather than present information.

2. Understand Paragraph Structure. Every well-written paragraph has purpose. The purpose may be to inform, define, explain, persuade, compare or contrast, illustrate, and so on. The purpose should always relate to the main idea and expand on it. As you read each paragraph, see how the body of the paragraph is used to tell you more about the main idea or topic sentence. Read the supporting details intelligently, recognizing that what you are reading is all designed to develop the single main idea.

Steps to Faster Reading

STEP 4: ORGANIZE FACTS

When you read, do you tend to see a lot of facts without any apparent connection or relationship? Understanding how the facts all fit together to deliver the author's message is, after all, the reason for reading. Good readers organize facts as they read. This helps them to read rapidly and well.

1. Discover the Writer's Plan. Look for a clue or signal word early in the article which might reveal the author's structure. Every writer has a plan or outline which he follows. If the reader can discover his method of organization, he has the key to understanding the message. Sometimes the author gives you obvious signals. If he says, "There are three reasons . . ." the wise reader looks for a listing of the three items. Other less obvious signal words such as *moreover, otherwise, consequently* all tell the reader the direction the writer's message will take.

2. Relate as You Read. As you read the selection, keep the information learned during the preview in mind. See how the ideas you are reading all fit into place. Consciously strive to relate what you are reading to the title. See how the author is carrying through in his attempt to piece together a meaningful message. As you discover the relationship among the ideas, the message comes through quickly and clearly.

Timed
Reading
Selections

Research Beneath the Sea

The ancient people who lived near the sea must have wondered what lay beneath its vast surface. As many as 24 centuries ago, a Mediterranean captain on a voyage to Egypt knew that when the plummet at the end of his ten-fathom sounding line reached a mud bottom, he was over the toe of the Nile's delta. Another day's travel should bring him within sight of a port at the delta's head. The navigator, with only a short sounding line for a tool, had learned something about the bottom of the Mediterranean Sea.

The marine geologist wants to know all that can be learned about the floors of the seas—a vast area covering about two-thirds of the earth's surface. This information will help serve mankind's practical needs. The efforts and talents of marine geologists will greatly expand the usefulness of the ocean floors.

The marine geologist compiles data about the topography or shape of the ocean floors, the location and character of the bottom sediments, the composition and structure of the underlying rocks, and the geological processes that have been at work during the eons of the sea floor's history. With this information the marine geologist may be able to assess the mineral resources of the sea floor and to predict and lessen the effects of certain hazards. Most of the tools and methods that make it possible to study the land beneath the ocean have been invented and developed within the past century. Parts of the ocean floor have now been mapped by echo soundings and other advanced methods. Underwater photographs, taken at great depths, show surface features such as outcrops of bedrock, rugged mountains, and deep canyons, with a greater total relief than the dry land.

With modern sampling methods, far more can be learned about the loose sediment on the ocean floor than was possible a half century ago. Although numerous random samples have been collected from the bottom of the seas in the last century, it was not until World War II that an account of the results obtained by an intensive study of core samples was published.

Cores are obtained by driving a metal tube into the bottom sediment, then drawing the tube up by cable and removing the core. Certain layers in these cores give information about geological history—for example, the relative dates of volcanic eruptions and periods of glaciation.

Recalling Facts

1. About how deep is the toe of the Nile Delta?
   - ☐ a. 5 fathoms
   - ☐ b. 10 fathoms
   - ☐ c. 15 fathoms

2. How much of the earth's surface is covered by water?
   - ☐ a. one-third
   - ☐ b. one-half
   - ☐ c. two-thirds

3. Marine geologists study the ocean's
   - ☐ a. vegetation.
   - ☐ b. animal life.
   - ☐ c. topography.

4. The ocean's floor has been mapped by
   - ☐ a. x-ray.
   - ☐ b. depth charges.
   - ☐ c. echo soundings.

5. What has aided in the understanding of underwater sediments?
   - ☐ a. cable laying
   - ☐ b. core sampling
   - ☐ c. marine photography

Understanding the Passage

6. This article is primarily about the
   - ☐ a. life processes which occur beneath the seas.
   - ☐ b. work of the marine geologist.
   - ☐ c. inventiveness of navigators.

7. One aspect of a marine geologist's work involves the
   - ☐ a. classification of fish and other sea life.
   - ☐ b. history of the earth's formation.
   - ☐ c. development of navigational techniques.

8. Most of the geologist's tools have been invented during the last
   - ☐ a. 10 years.
   - ☐ b. 45 years.
   - ☐ c. 100 years.

9. The author creates interest in his subject by using
   - ☐ a. a great many facts concerning the oceans of the world.
   - ☐ b. precise argument in conjunction with strong criticism.
   - ☐ c. interesting description with historical background.

10. We can conclude that
    - ☐ a. marine geology is a specialized field.
    - ☐ b. the sea is teeming with millions of life forms.
    - ☐ c. ships are now equipped with sonar and radar.

Some household pests have an amazing ability to escape extinction. Cockroaches, for example, which have been on the earth millions of years longer than humans, can live on any kind of food. They thrive in all parts of the world. Some types of cockroaches prefer man's home to other habitats. Once they enter it, they use many instinctive tricks to keep from being found.

Systematic housecleaning can help control household pests. A home can be free of practically all pests by a combination of continuous good housekeeping and the proper use of the right pesticide at the right time.

It is easier to prevent pests from infesting a home than it is to get rid of them after they are in. Household pests seek available food, and places where they may hide and breed. If these attractions are eliminated, the pests will look elsewhere for them.

Many household pests live on spilled food and organic matter that has not been completely cleaned up. They breed, multiply, and hide in small cracks and crevices in cupboards, walls, and floors. They hide in seldom used storage cabinets, behind washtubs, and around water pipes and toilets.

Frequent scrubbing with hot water and soap or detergent will keep these places clean.

Garbage, bits of food, crumbs, scraps of fabrics, lint, and other waste materials that pests may eat or that they may breed in must be promptly discarded.

All foods must be kept in tightly closed containers that are as clean outside as they are inside. Before purchasing dry foods, one should examine the packages carefully for evidence of breaks and insect infestation.

Cockroaches and silverfish often enter the house in the crevices of cardboard cartons used in transporting groceries or other materials. These containers should not be left in the kitchen or basement where the pests may escape.

Any place where pests may enter should be sealed. The openings and cracks around wash basins, toilet bowls, water pipes, drain pipes, and radiator pipes must be caulked. Cracks around baseboards and between floorboards should be filled in and openings where rats or mice may enter should be covered. Windows and doors should be tight fitting.

Pest prevention measures should be practiced at all times. Application of pesticide may be needed to supplement good housekeeping. The directions on the pesticide label must be followed carefully. Pesticides contain dangerous ingredients and should be used with caution.

Recalling Facts

1. Silverfish often enter a house
   - ☐ a. in fresh fruit.
   - ☐ b. on shoes.
   - ☐ c. in cardboard cartons.

2. The author advises the homeowner to
   - ☐ a. caulk cracks.
   - ☐ b. set traps.
   - ☐ c. spray foundations.

3. An insect that can live on any food is the
   - ☐ a. ant.
   - ☐ b. earwig.
   - ☐ c. cockroach.

4. According to the author, insects will not live in an area washed with
   - ☐ a. alcohol.
   - ☐ b. chemicals.
   - ☐ c. soap and water.

5. To prevent insect infestation, foods should be kept in
   - ☐ a. warm places.
   - ☐ b. lighted areas.
   - ☐ c. closed containers.

Understanding the Passage

6. Which common expression applies to this article?
   - ☐ a. An ounce of prevention is worth a pound of cure.
   - ☐ b. Don't count your chickens until they're hatched.
   - ☐ c. A penny saved is a penny earned.

7. The author implies that
   - ☐ a. ants are attracted to grease and sugar.
   - ☐ b. cockroaches are difficult to kill.
   - ☐ c. silverfish eat paper and cloth.

8. According to the author,
   - ☐ a. rats and mice prefer cheese to other foods.
   - ☐ b. pesticides should never be used in the home.
   - ☐ c. insects don't usually breed in clean areas.

9. In the article, the cockroach is described as
   - ☐ a. clever.
   - ☐ b. dangerous.
   - ☐ c. selective.

10. We can conclude that
    - ☐ a. invasions of most household insects can be prevented.
    - ☐ b. some tropical insects are poisonous.
    - ☐ c. many states sponsor pest-control programs.

3 Food Additives

We can get along without food additives, but not very well. Were it not for food additives, we would have to go back to the old idea of bakery freshness—good today, stale tomorrow.

Many adults remember when the cottage cheese separated, cookies dried up in two days, any food with fat or oil in it became rancid, canned vegetables and fruits were soft and mushy, and marshmallows got too hard to toast. Without additives, the variety and quality of foods would return to those familiar to grandmother. The quantities available would definitely be less, and quick foods would not exist.

Some people have called these additives poisonous chemicals. If all chemicals are poisonous, then people should stop eating, because all foods are chemicals. Some common additives are pure chemicals, such as the potassium iodide in table salt and many familiar vitamins that are all essential to man's health.

Expressing foods in chemical terms can be a lengthy job. For example, milk is made of water, fats, proteins, lactose, salts, acids, pigments, enzymes, vitamins, and gases. Milk is a wonderful chemical, but hardly poisonous.

Many allowable food additives are taken directly from food itself. For example, lecithin is found in all living things. It is obtained mostly from soybeans and is used as an emulsifier to keep ingredients in processed foods from separating.

A large number of laboratory-created additives are also found naturally in foods. Calcium and sodium propionate, for example, are made during fermentation in the production of Swiss cheese. The propionates help to prevent mold. They are used primarily in baked goods. The vitamins used to improve the nutritive value of many foods are identical to the vitamins found naturally in food. Actually, all additives are chemicals, and the body cannot tell between them.

The cost of an additive does not increase the cost of a food. For example, enough calcium propionate to help protect 1,000 loaves of bread from becoming moldy costs less than ten cents.

In addition to these additives, there are also incidental additives that have no planned function in food but become a part of it during some phase of processing, packaging, or storing.

Good examples are substances that might get into the food from a packaging material. The safety of incidental additives is scientifically controlled as are the other additives. A food additive must be of some benefit to a food or its production.

Recalling Facts

1. Food additives generally prevent
   - ☐ a. staleness.
   - ☐ b. illness.
   - ☐ c. poor nutrition.

2. Without preservatives, cottage cheese would
   - ☐ a. separate.
   - ☐ b. sour.
   - ☐ c. harden.

3. The author says that foods must be classified as
   - ☐ a. fuels.
   - ☐ b. calories.
   - ☐ c. chemicals.

4. Potassium iodide is found in
   - ☐ a. aspirin.
   - ☐ b. salt.
   - ☐ c. sugar.

5. According to the author, propionates prevent
   - ☐ a. thinning.
   - ☐ b. mushiness.
   - ☐ c. mold formation.

Understanding the Passage

6. The author is critical of
   - ☐ a. people who eat too much food with additives.
   - ☐ b. companies that use chemicals to preserve food.
   - ☐ c. people who feel that additives are poisonous.

7. For the most part, food additives are
   - ☐ a. costly.
   - ☐ b. unnecessary.
   - ☐ c. inexpensive.

8. Incidental additives are
   - ☐ a. put into food before processing.
   - ☐ b. of no benefit to food.
   - ☐ c. high in vitamin content.

9. The author mentions marshmallows as an example of a food that
   - ☐ a. has several preservatives.
   - ☐ b. needs no preservatives.
   - ☐ c. spoils without preservatives.

10. The reader can conclude that
    - ☐ a. most additives are safe to eat.
    - ☐ b. most additives are organic by nature.
    - ☐ c. several additives are toxic in large quantities.

Potatoes are produced in every state, but about half of the commercial crop is grown in Idaho, Maine, California, and Washington.

Most of our year-round supply of fresh potatoes is harvested in September or October. These fall crop potatoes are stored from one to nine months before shipment to retail outlets.

Many potatoes, however, are freshly harvested and marketed from January through September. These are called "new" potatoes. This term is also used to describe freshly dug fall potatoes that are not fully matured.

Most harvesting is done by potato combines that dig the potatoes out of the ground and move them up a conveyor that shakes them, allows soil to drop through, and conveys the potatoes directly into containers or trucks. Usually several workers on the combine pick out any vines, stones, or other debris. A few harvesters also have built-in devices for removing debris.

Potatoes are usually brushed or washed at the packinghouse. Dirty potatoes are unattractive, and the dirt itself contributes to the weight for which the buyer is paying.

After they are cleaned, potatoes are mechanically sized and are then sorted into grades by packinghouse workers. The potatoes are packed according to grade and size. The grade is often certified during packing by federal or state inspectors.

Over 40 percent of the fresh potatoes are now marketed at retail stores in consumer unit packages. Common types of bags are film, open mesh, paper with mesh or film window, or plain paper. The trend is toward packing so the shopper can see the contents.

Potatoes may be packaged in consumer units at the packinghouse or at wholesale houses in city terminal markets. Retail chains also do a good deal of packing in consumer units in their central warehouses.

Packing is largely mechanized, and bags are generally check-weighed afterward to ensure that they are slightly overweight and thus allow for shrinkage in marketing.

Red potatoes and some white varieties are sometimes treated with colored or clear wax before shipment in order to improve their appearance. The Food and Drug Administration requires that potatoes so treated must be plainly marked. Under the Federal Food, Drug, and Cosmetic Act, it is illegal to color white potatoes red or to use colored wax to make potatoes appear fresher or of better quality. In response, several producing states have banned all use of artificial color.

Recalling Facts

1. Potatoes are grown in
   - a. a few states.
   - b. most states.
   - c. every state.

2. One of the leading potato states is
   - a. Arkansas.
   - b. Maine.
   - c. Michigan.

3. Most of the year-round supply of potatoes is harvested during
   - a. August.
   - b. October.
   - c. December.

4. How long are some potatoes stored before shipment to markets?
   - a. two weeks
   - b. nine months
   - c. one year

5. Fall potatoes that are not fully mature are called
   - a. green potatoes.
   - b. harvest potatoes.
   - c. new potatoes.

Understanding the Passage

6. The author implies that packers are careful about the
   - a. weight of packaged potatoes.
   - b. shape of potatoes.
   - c. wrapper used on packaged potatoes.

7. Almost half of the potatoes sold are purchased by the consumer
   - a. in transparent bags.
   - b. from open bins.
   - c. in consumer unit packages.

8. The article suggests that as potatoes age, they
   - a. shed some of their weight.
   - b. take on a more subtle flavor.
   - c. become a lighter color.

9. Several potato-producing states have
   - a. required the use of transparent packages for potatoes.
   - b. banned the use of artificial color in potatoes.
   - c. outlawed the use of wax on potatoes.

10. The reader can conclude that potatoes
    - a. are least expensive during the winter months.
    - b. are still dug by hand on most large farms.
    - c. grow best in cool climates.

Colorful names and colorful places are a part of the farflung system of the national wildlife refuges. The system is a chain of nature preserves that includes more than 300 units totaling nearly 29 million acres. There's a refuge in all but five of the fifty states.

Many refuges lie near the busy urban stretches of the eastern seaboard, the Midwest, and the Pacific coast. They mainly offer sanctuary to millions of migrating waterfowl, but they also have other values. People need solitude, too, and millions of Americans find respite and recreation when visiting these wildlife havens that can also be human refuges.

Most people come to observe the birds or to merely wander around and momentarily escape the tension of city living. Others satisfy a recreational thirst for hunting, fishing, or boating.

Several refuges are unique because they make up the last stronghold for animals bordering on extinction. An example is the Aransas Refuge, located halfway down the Texas coast. Here, on 47,000 acres of bays, estuaries, tidal flats, and sandy islands, visitors may see the whooping crane, one of our largest birds and probably the rarest in North America.

This giant of a bird, standing 5 feet high and with a 7-foot wingspread, winters only on Aransas and the nearby lands. Cranes and many other types of wildlife are there from late October to mid-April, when each whooper begins its hazardous 2,600-mile trip to summer nesting grounds in the far north.

The only known whooping crane nesting area is in Wood Buffalo National Park of Canada's Northwest Territories.

Whooping cranes had all but vanished from the wildlife scene before establishment of Aransas. Fifteen lone survivors were reported during the winter of 1941-42, and things continued to be "touch and go" for the species for a number of years. The winter of 1965-66 saw 44 individuals on the refuge—and today the population is slowly but surely edging upwards.

The Key deer is another species that had also dwindled to near extinction in the 1940s but has since been preserved for people to see. A remnant herd of 50 animals was faced with certain displacement—victims of intensive land development—when area purchases to keep their habitat were started. The population of Key deer numbers over 400 animals today, most of them living in the refuge lands on Big Pine Key in Florida. This increase is due mainly to the refuge's protection.

Recalling Facts

1. About how many million acres comprise the National Wildlife refuges?
   - ☐ a. 10
   - ☐ b. 20
   - ☐ c. 30

2. How many states have wildlife refuges?
   - ☐ a. 25
   - ☐ b. 35
   - ☐ c. 45

3. Wildlife refuges offer sanctuary to millions of
   - ☐ a. birds.
   - ☐ b. elk.
   - ☐ c. bears.

4. Which one of the following is not cited as a major activity of refuges?
   - ☐ a. hunting
   - ☐ b. fishing
   - ☐ c. camping

5. The Aransas Refuge is located on the coast of
   - ☐ a. Florida.
   - ☐ b. Texas.
   - ☐ c. Georgia.

Understanding the Passage

6. The author talks extensively about the
   - ☐ a. North American bald eagle.
   - ☐ b. American plains bison.
   - ☐ c. whooping crane.

7. The Key deer is mentioned in the article as an example of
   - ☐ a. a type of deer hunted extensively in Florida.
   - ☐ b. an animal that must be controlled carefully.
   - ☐ c. an animal saved from extinction by refuges.

8. This article is primarily concerned with the
   - ☐ a. planning of national wildlife refuges.
   - ☐ b. tracking and counting of rare animals.
   - ☐ c. function of wildlife refuges.

9. The article implies that wildlife sanctuaries
   - ☐ a. are located mostly in swampy areas.
   - ☐ b. can be found in all parts of the country.
   - ☐ c. have been established only along coastal areas.

10. We may conclude that
    - ☐ a. wildlife refuges cater to rare animals only.
    - ☐ b. most people go to refuges seeking peace and quiet.
    - ☐ c. tax money is not used to support wildlife refuges.

Industrial safety does not just happen. Companies with low accident rates plan their safety programs, work hard to organize them, and continue working to keep them alive and active. When the work is well done, a climate of accident-free operations is established where time lost due to injuries is kept at a minimum.

Successful safety programs may differ greatly in the emphasis placed on certain aspects of the program. Some place great emphasis on mechanical guarding. Others stress safe work practices by following rules or regulations covering working conditions. Still others depend on an emotional appeal to the worker. But, there are certain basic ideas that must be used in every program if maximum results are to be obtained.

Every plant needs a safety program designed for its specific need. Surveys have shown that the highest injury frequency rates are often found in the medium-sized plants, those with from 50 to 500 employees. Somewhat better rates are often found in small plants, fewer than 50 employees. Large plants, with 500 or more employees, tend to have the best rate. However, the need for a safety plan exists regardless of size.

Small companies, because of their closer relationship between management and worker, can conduct an accident prevention program with a few organizational details. Such a program can usually operate with a part-time safety director.

There can be no question about the value of a safety program. From a financial standpoint alone, safety pays off. The fewer the injury claims, the better the workmen's insurance rate. This may mean the difference between operating at a profit or at a loss.

There are other intangible benefits. Operating costs can be reduced because of less damage to equipment and product. Production increases because people can work without the fear of injury. These are tangible benefits that make everyone happy.

Less tangible benefits are a direct result of a successful safety program. A plant with a poor accident record does not attract or hold the best workers. On the other hand, a clean, safe plant creates the climate where good work habits can be cultivated. A safety program will help to attract good workers and to conserve their skills. A safe plant is a well-organized plant that soon becomes known as a good place to work. Management's attitude toward its workers is seen in such a plant. And the result is good public relations.

Recalling Facts

1. Medium-sized plants contain no more than
   - ☐ a. 500 workers.
   - ☐ b. 1,000 workers.
   - ☐ c. 1,500 workers.

2. The highest injury frequency rates are found in plants of
   - ☐ a. small size.
   - ☐ b. medium size.
   - ☐ c. large size.

3. Safety programs in plants of all sizes tend to
   - ☐ a. increase costs.
   - ☐ b. decrease costs.
   - ☐ c. keep costs the same.

4. A part-time safety director should be hired in a
   - ☐ a. small plant.
   - ☐ b. medium-sized plant.
   - ☐ c. large plant.

5. The cost of workmen's compensation insurance is often based on
   - ☐ a. plant location.
   - ☐ b. basic salary.
   - ☐ c. injury statistics.

Understanding the Passage

6. The author describes a safe plant as one with
   - ☐ a. positive management activities.
   - ☐ b. flexible scheduling.
   - ☐ c. advanced production concepts.

7. The author implies that
   - ☐ a. plant safety occurs naturally from careful work.
   - ☐ b. many factories are unwilling to try safety programs.
   - ☐ c. accident-free operations must be well planned.

8. The author suggests that large plants
   - ☐ a. are more aware of safety needs.
   - ☐ b. regard safety as an outgrowth of strict discipline.
   - ☐ c. post safety regulations at all building exits.

9. This selection could be titled
   - ☐ a. Increasing Production Through Safety.
   - ☐ b. Improving Working Conditions.
   - ☐ c. Mechanical Safety Procedures in Manufacturing.

10. We can conclude that
    - ☐ a. the federal government pays for many safety programs.
    - ☐ b. safety programs are beneficial to plants of all sizes.
    - ☐ c. products reflect the cost of safety programs.

7 The Human Side of Washington

The picture of George Washington as a cold, distant figure and a model of great virtue is a misconception that has tended to obscure his vigor, his wide-ranging interests, his kindness, and the warmth of his personality. Many stories survive that reveal the human side of Washington. Elkanah Watson, a merchant adventurer who came to Mount Vernon on business, went to bed with a cold and a cough. During the night he was surprised to see Washington himself, standing at his bedside with a bowl of hot tea in his hand.

On another occasion, several young men visiting at Mount Vernon were on the lawn playing "pitch the bar," the ancient sport in which contestants throw a heavy bar toward a mark. Washington strolled up and, without removing his coat, picked up a bar and threw it with all his strength. Smiling, he walked away, saying, "When you beat my pitch, young gentlemen, I'll try again."

As a soldier he was a rigid disciplinarian. But there is an account which relates that on mild days at Valley Forge he went out and pitched ball with his young aides or, as one officer said, "did us the honor to play at wickets with us." When occasion allowed, he enjoyed sitting long after dinner to gossip with his military family over hazelnuts and wine. And from the farmhouse near Middlebrook, where the army wintered in 1778, General Nathanael Greene wrote a friend, "We had a little dance at my quarters a few evenings past. His Excellency and Mrs. Greene danced upwards of three hours without sitting down. Upon the whole, we had a pretty little frisk."

If the ladies found the General sometimes preoccupied, they also found him pleasantly familiar and witty. Mrs. Theodorick Bland, visiting the army at Morristown when Mrs. Washington was wintering with the General, wrote her sister-in-law: "We visit them frequently. From dinner till night he is free. His worthy lady seems to be in perfect felicity, while she is by the side of her 'Old Man' as she calls him. We often make parties on horseback, the General, His Lady, and his aides-de-camp. Generally, General Washington throws off the hero and takes on the chatty agreeable companion. He can be downright impudent, sometimes, such impudence, Fanny, as you and I like."

Washington valued a sense of humor and enjoyed the relaxing times that he spent with friends.

Recalling Facts

1. Elkanah Watson was
   - ☐ a. an artist.
   - ☐ b. a diplomat.
   - ☐ c. a merchant.

2. Washington's cure for a bad cold was
   - ☐ a. orange juice.
   - ☐ b. cold soup.
   - ☐ c. hot tea.

3. The author describes the game of wickets as
   - ☐ a. ball pitching.
   - ☐ b. boat rowing.
   - ☐ c. horse riding.

4. General Nathanael Greene wrote to a friend about Washington's
   - ☐ a. swearing.
   - ☐ b. dancing.
   - ☐ c. singing.

5. Mrs. Washington often called her husband
   - ☐ a. Father.
   - ☐ b. General.
   - ☐ c. Old Man.

Understanding the Passage

6. The author's purpose is to
   - ☐ a. show that Washington was an intellectual.
   - ☐ b. support the belief that Washington was cold and distant.
   - ☐ c. prove that Washington was a friendly individual.

7. The author mentions the incident with Elkanah Watson as an example of Washington's
   - ☐ a. kindness.
   - ☐ b. self-sacrifice.
   - ☐ c. boastfulness.

8. Several young men visiting at Mount Vernon witnessed Washington's
   - ☐ a. fitful temper.
   - ☐ b. modest concern.
   - ☐ c. unusual strength.

9. We can assume that
   - ☐ a. most military men had little respect for Washington.
   - ☐ b. Mrs. Washington accompanied her husband on some missions.
   - ☐ c. Washington did not believe in slavery.

10. As a soldier, Washington would not allow any of his
   - ☐ a. men to break the rules.
   - ☐ b. friends to enter the combat zone.
   - ☐ c. men to play games in camp.

When rain falls or when water runs downhill on bare soil, it moves soil particles, organic matter, and soluble nutrients. This moving is soil erosion.

Soil erosion by water may occur anywhere there is enough rain to cause runoff, or where land is flooded by irrigation, melting snow, or other causes. To avoid erosion, the soil must be protected from moving water. Dense vegetation, such as cover crops, mulches, grasses, or trees, will intercept rain and snow runoff. Where tillage leaves the soil exposed, barriers like terraces or sown strips of different crops can help control runoff. Otherwise, tillage needs to be confined to nearly level soils where water moves slowly.

Land used for grazing or wood crops may also be eroded by water if the soil is exposed because of heavy grazing or careless cutting and burning. But with good management, grasslands and woodlands are usually safe from erosion.

Erosion by water has already damaged much of the farmland in the United States. Some soils that are so badly damaged they cannot be restored, or soils inherently unsuited for cultivation, need to be converted to other uses.

When soils are kept in cultivation, the prevention of excessive erosion is important. Erosion control requires the attention of each farmer to his land acre by acre. It also requires cooperation between farmers on adjoining land, for water knows no property boundaries.

Erosion goes on all the time. Normal erosion occurs where water, wind, or other erosive agents remove soil or rock from slopes that have not been disturbed by man. This is called geologic erosion.

In arid and semiarid regions these processes are rapid and erratic. Infrequent but torrential rains carve the hills and scour the valleys. The sparse vegetation offers little protection. The result is a landscape of angular forms. Flat-topped mesas and concave slopes are characteristic.

In humid and subhumid regions, the soil is held in place by dense forests and prairies. Here, normal erosion is usually less rapid than soil formation. Hilltops are rounded and slopes are gently curved. Sharp angles and straight lines in the landscape are unusual.

The first settlers found the land in general equilibrium with the climate. But as they cleared away the vegetation to grow crops, cut the timber, or let their livestock overgraze the grasslands, erosion speeded up. It is this accelerated or man-made erosion that we are concerned with in today's agriculture.

Recalling Facts

1. What can be used to prevent water erosion?
   - ☐ a. grass
   - ☐ b. fences
   - ☐ c. buildings

2. Tillage should be confined to
   - ☐ a. soft soils.
   - ☐ b. dry land.
   - ☐ c. level ground.

3. The author points out that erosion in well-managed woodlands is
   - ☐ a. impossible.
   - ☐ b. likely.
   - ☐ c. unusual.

4. Erosion control is the responsibility of
   - ☐ a. land developers.
   - ☐ b. individual farmers.
   - ☐ c. the United States government.

5. Erosion that occurs on slopes undisturbed by man is called
   - ☐ a. natural erosion.
   - ☐ b. regional erosion.
   - ☐ c. geologic erosion.

Understanding the Passage

6. Angular landforms occur when
   - ☐ a. rainfall is frequent and heavy.
   - ☐ b. vegetation is dense and protective.
   - ☐ c. rain falls quickly in dry areas.

7. The author implies that
   - ☐ a. heavy grazing increases the risk of erosion.
   - ☐ b. forest fires help to prevent erosion.
   - ☐ c. erosion can be controlled by cultivation.

8. Erosion by water is less likely in
   - ☐ a. humid and subhumid regions.
   - ☐ b. desert areas.
   - ☐ c. farming localities.

9. The author implies that man-made erosion in the United States began with
   - ☐ a. erratic climate changes.
   - ☐ b. the first settlers.
   - ☐ c. the increase in farming in recent years.

10. We can conclude that
   - ☐ a. soil erosion is a major concern of the Agriculture Department.
   - ☐ b. man's actions can speed up the processes of erosion.
   - ☐ c. wind erosion is not a problem in the United States.

A Shining Beacon

The Statue of Liberty was declared a national monument by President Calvin Coolidge on October 15, 1924. The boundaries of the monument were set at the outer edge of old Fort Wood.

On August 3, 1956, a joint resolution of the Congress approved the change of the island's name to Liberty Island. This was done in recognition of the special importance of the Statue and of the plan to construct at its base, within the walls of old Fort Wood, the American Museum of Immigration. This museum honors all those who came to this land in search of freedom and opportunity and to whom the Statue of Liberty was a shining beacon.

While Liberty Island, with an area of about 12 acres, is located in the upper bay of New York Harbor, it is geographically in the territorial waters of New Jersey. Liberty Island is almost three-eighths of a mile offshore from Jersey City, New Jersey, its source of telephone, power, and water services. It is about one and five-eighths miles from the Battery, at the southern tip of Manhattan Island, New York City. Transportation and mail services are provided by boat from the Battery. At present a privately owned ferry line is operating under contract with the government.

The monument is open daily, Sundays and holidays included, from 9 A.M. to 5 P.M. Souvenirs, postcards, and food are provided through the facilities of a private concessioner. Postal and telephone facilities are also available. Seatwalls are provided on the grounds and there are benches along the walk around the statue. Monument personnel are on duty and will be glad to answer any questions.

There are a number of interpreters in the lobby of the administration building, as well as historical and interpretive markers along the pedestal passageway beyond the elevator shaft. More historical and interpretive markers are on the fourth level at the top of the elevator shaft. Outside, along the railings of the overlook, a series of sketch drawings show in silhouette the scene directly in front of the viewer. The drawings identify various features and buildings of New York Harbor and the skyline. By the use of these sketch drawings, one may identify practically all of the points of interest that can be seen from the four sides of the overlook, with its magnificent panoramic view of New York Harbor, Manhattan Island, Staten Island, and the New Jersey waterfront.

Recalling Facts

1. The Statue of Liberty was declared a national monument in the middle
   - ☐ a. 1920s.
   - ☐ b. 1930s.
   - ☐ c. 1940s.

2. Liberty Island was formerly called
   - ☐ a. Fort Adams.
   - ☐ b. Fort Kent.
   - ☐ c. Fort Wood.

3. Liberty Island occupies a total of
   - ☐ a. 5 acres.
   - ☐ b. 12 acres.
   - ☐ c. 19 acres.

4. The ferry line that serves the Statue is operated by
   - ☐ a. a private owner.
   - ☐ b. New York City.
   - ☐ c. the Federal Government.

5. At the base of the Statue is a museum honoring
   - ☐ a. former Presidents.
   - ☐ b. great athletes.
   - ☐ c. immigrants.

Understanding the Passage

6. The author states that the Statue of Liberty
   - ☐ a. was a gift from France.
   - ☐ b. was damaged during World War II.
   - ☐ c. is open every day year-round.

7. In the Statue of Liberty a visitor can find
   - ☐ a. an impressive library.
   - ☐ b. signs printed in several languages.
   - ☐ c. a collection of Presidential letters.

8. The Statue's power, telephone, and water services originate in
   - ☐ a. New York City.
   - ☐ b. New York State.
   - ☐ c. New Jersey.

9. According to the author, the Statue of Liberty symbolizes
   - ☐ a. freedom.
   - ☐ b. justice.
   - ☐ c. wealth.

10. We can conclude that the
    - ☐ a. Statue of Liberty attracts tourists.
    - ☐ b. arm of the Statue has been closed to tourists.
    - ☐ c. United Nations Building is situated next to the Statue.

Scientists now tend to agree that the noise level for potential hearing loss begins at about 70 decibels. Some of them are very concerned because normal daily life often exposes people to noise levels of about 70 decibels even inside their homes. Cities have always been noisy, but noise is now spreading to areas that were quiet just a few years ago.

Clearly, something must be done or noise will seriously and permanently maim the population. Fortunately, the knowledge and methods to control noise already exist. As a matter of fact, this is one instance where the knowledge of control methods exceeds the knowledge about the effects on human life and on the environment.

There are two common means for control. The first is reducing noise at its source, and the second is changing the sound path by distance or by shielding.

The second approach is being used more often today as people become more aware of the danger of noise. New building codes require better sound insulation in homes and apartments. More and more towns are passing zoning ordinances that try to segregate noisy factories or airports from residential areas. Sound-absorbent materials and construction designed to block sound paths are slowly coming into use in offices and homes. New highways are being built to redirect traffic noise up and away from nearby areas. Aircraft are increasingly being required to use reduced-power flights around airports.

There are many examples of available noise control methods that are not being used. More flexible building codes would permit the use of quieter kinds of plumbing pipes. Sound-absorbing materials can reduce the noise of motors and engines. Power generators can be quieted with baffles, exhaust silencers, and sound absorbers. Truck tires can be made with quieter treads. In many cases, the cost of building quieter machines is the same or only slightly higher than that of the current noisy ones. Even though the new equipment may cost more initially, it can prove more profitable in the long run. The new jumbo jets, for example, are quieter than the older ones, yet they are more powerful and carry twice as many passengers.

All of these methods are only partial measures as noise levels continue to rise. Most specialists in the field agree that much of the solution must come from eliminating some of the noise at its source, therefore saving through prevention the large costs of hearing loss.

Recalling Facts

1. The noise level for possible hearing loss begins at about
   - ☐ a. 30 decibels.
   - ☐ b. 70 decibels.
   - ☐ c. 100 decibels.

2. The technology needed to control noise
   - ☐ a. is now available.
   - ☐ b. is being developed.
   - ☐ c. will be available soon.

3. Jet pilots are being advised to land
   - ☐ a. on longer runways.
   - ☐ b. with reduced power.
   - ☐ c. after dark.

4. The author discusses several aspects of
   - ☐ a. installing quieter plumbing.
   - ☐ b. building better motors.
   - ☐ c. shielding against noise.

5. How many practical means for controlling noise does the author present?
   - ☐ a. two
   - ☐ b. three
   - ☐ c. four

Understanding the Passage

6. The author strongly implies that
   - ☐ a. deafening noises are common in everyday life.
   - ☐ b. the city today is quieter than it was fifty years ago.
   - ☐ c. noise pollution is more serious than water pollution.

7. The reader can assume that airports of the future will
   - ☐ a. have runways in a north-south pattern.
   - ☐ b. be located in unpopulated areas.
   - ☐ c. be required to warn passengers of high noise levels.

8. Many people who should be concerned about noise problems
   - ☐ a. own large corporations.
   - ☐ b. reject all federal assistance.
   - ☐ c. are indifferent to the situation.

9. Jumbo jets are mentioned as examples of
   - ☐ a. efficient transportation with low levels of noise.
   - ☐ b. vehicles that cause serious air pollution.
   - ☐ c. scientific advances that do more harm than good.

10. The author develops the ideas in the selection with
    - ☐ a. carefully chosen facts.
    - ☐ b. persuasive opinions.
    - ☐ c. personal interviews.

11   Camping: Americans See Nature

Forest campgrounds grow more popular each year with experienced, as well as amateur, campers. To visitors, the Forest Service says, "Welcome to the National Forests—yours to enjoy, protect, keep clean!" This is the Forest Service's way of asking the cooperation of the one visitor in a thousand who might misuse or damage tables, signs, or other structures. Dollars saved by lowering repair and replacement costs can be used to build new recreation areas in order to accommodate the increasing numbers of Americans using the forests.

If you've never camped, join those thousands who this year will camp in the woods for the first time. Get the advice of an experienced woodsman, • or study camping magazines and books. Then plan a simple trip—don't be too ambitious your first time out—and head for the woods. The campers you'll meet will be friendly and glad to share their woods lore.

Really experienced campers prefer to simply throw packs on their backs and head into backcountry—the wilder parts of the National Forest system. There they try to recapture the pioneer spirit of their forefathers by fending for themselves.

Hikers explore old trails and beat their way across country, making • camp whenever day ends. Horse riders travel wilderness trails, sleep beneath the stars, and return to civilization refreshed. Fishermen trek to remote streams and high-country lakes, and hunters search the hills for the next winter's venison and bear steaks. Families, too, enjoy the get-away-from-it-all experience of primitive travel and deep woods camping.

To help backcountry campers, the Forest Service has blazed miles of trails and provided crude campsites—a few with three-sided shelters and fire pits.

The supreme camping experience for many people is a wilderness trip. No roads cross the wilderness and no motorized vehicles are allowed. The only trails are for horse riders and hikers. Some of the better known areas, • where popular use has made it necessary to provide sanitation and safety, have a few special campsites with simple facilities.

Backcountry camping deep in a wilderness requires careful planning and proper equipment. Before heading into the wilds, study a detailed map of the area and learn the terrain. Plan menus and select equipment carefully to keep loads light for horses and backpackers. Carry a first aid kit for emergencies. And always have a map and compass to keep you on trail.

Recalling Facts

1. All that the Forest Service expects from campers is
   ☐ a. caution.
   ☐ b. friendliness.
   ☐ c. cooperation.

2. Statistics show that destruction is caused by one camper in
   ☐ a. ten.
   ☐ b. a hundred.
   ☐ c. a thousand.

3. The article states that most campers are
   ☐ a. careless.
   ☐ b. experienced.
   ☐ c. friendly.

4. Camping sites tend to be
   ☐ a. primitive.
   ☐ b. luxurious.
   ☐ c. modern.

5. Backcountry trails provide no
   ☐ a. sanitary facilities.
   ☐ b. roads.
   ☐ c. campsites.

Understanding the Passage

6. Regarding fire, the article implies that
   ☐ a. forest fires destroy many good camping trails yearly.
   ☐ b. food may be cooked in fire pits on some trails.
   ☐ c. campfires are not allowed in National Forests.

7. This article states that money not spent on the repair of campsites
   ☐ a. may be used for the construction of new schools.
   ☐ b. may be spent on new recreational facilities.
   ☐ c. can be applied to the publication of camping magazines.

8. The author advises first-time campers not to
   ☐ a. expect help from experienced campers.
   ☐ b. carry backpacks.
   ☐ c. plan long trips.

9. The primary motivation behind camping probably lies in
   ☐ a. the spirit of conquest.
   ☐ b. a need for exercise.
   ☐ c. the challenge of survival.

10. Most campers apparently prefer
    ☐ a. scenic trails.
    ☐ b. rugged trails.
    ☐ c. mountain paths.

Long before ecology was in the forefront of many minds, NASA was genuinely concerned about aircraft noise. But the supersonic transport program did more to focus attention on noise problems than any other single factor.

There are two basic areas where noise from an aircraft is a problem. The first is in the immediate vicinity of airports, in areas that lie under the usual approach and departure paths of jet transports. The second is on the ground anywhere under the flight path of any plane traveling at supersonic speed. These two problems are different and demand completely different approaches and solutions.

In some ways, aircraft noise is the unwitting creation of the passengers. More people want to travel and the best solution is to make larger and faster aircraft. Bigger and faster transports demand more power and more installed thrust. More power means more noise, and there hasn't been much of an alternative until recently.

The first attempt to reduce noise on the ground under departure paths was to change the nature of those paths. Shortly after takeoff, the pilot reduces power while he maintains a constant-altitude flight over residential areas. Once clear of the urban area, he increases power to climb to an assigned altitude.

But this is only a temporary solution to remove some of the burden from those living next to the runways. A better solution is to make engines quieter.

Studies have shown that the major noise annoyance from jet engines centers on the screaming sound of turbofan engines. The fans that give this class of engine its name also give it a characteristic whine.

NASA decided on a two-step solution to the problem. First, research would be done on current engine installations, changing them to reduce their noise. Second, a new design for a basically quieter engine would be developed.

Acoustic absorptive materials were installed in the inlet and exhaust areas of the jet engines. Additional rings of the material were placed in the engine inlets. The results were dramatic. Noise levels were reduced substantially. In some cases, the reduction in a four-engine aircraft was greater than that obtained by shutting down three of four untreated engines. Jet engines with acceptable noise levels can be available technically.

Modification is, at best, only temporary and is limited by pre-existing conditions and designs. The ideal approach is to design a quiet engine from the beginning.

Recalling Facts

1. The author blames aircraft noise ultimately on
   - ☐ a. designers.
   - ☐ b. pilots.
   - ☐ c. passengers.

2. Aircraft noise is the result of
   - ☐ a. thrust.
   - ☐ b. imbalance.
   - ☐ c. altitude.

3. The major noise problem from jets centers on
   - ☐ a. injection engines.
   - ☐ b. turbofan engines.
   - ☐ c. hydrofoil engines.

4. The author describes the noise of jet engines as
   - ☐ a. a whine.
   - ☐ b. a roar.
   - ☐ c. an explosion.

5. One area where aircraft noise is a problem is
   - ☐ a. in cities.
   - ☐ b. under flight paths.
   - ☐ c. at airports.

Understanding the Passage

6. Over urban areas, planes fly at
   - ☐ a. low altitudes.
   - ☐ b. assigned altitudes.
   - ☐ c. high altitudes.

7. NASA's work on insulating materials has cut jet noise by
   - ☐ a. one-fourth.
   - ☐ b. one-half.
   - ☐ c. three-fourths.

8. The long-range solution to noisy jets is
   - ☐ a. higher quality absorptive materials.
   - ☐ b. better engine design.
   - ☐ c. fewer moving parts.

9. According to the author, NASA was working on jet noise
   - ☐ a. while it was planning satellite launches.
   - ☐ b. before many countries had commercial jet service.
   - ☐ c. long before noise pollution was considered a problem.

10. We can conclude that the problem of noise pollution
    - ☐ a. will be solved in the near future.
    - ☐ b. has been solved by NASA researchers.
    - ☐ c. will not be solved for many years.

13   Cruising in the Caribbean

Since the census of 1970, the resident population of the Virgin Islands has jumped from 62,468 to over 96,000, including alien workers and part-time residents. The majority of the residents are descendents of the slaves who worked on the old Danish plantations, and persons of French origin who migrated many years ago from the French West Indies. The rest of the population is of Danish, Spanish, Scotch, and Portuguese descent, with an ever-increasing influx of persons from the United States mainland and nearby Puerto Rico. English is the traditional language of the Virgin Islands. French is spoken by some of the citizens of French descent and Spanish by the Puerto Ricans. The populace is religious and embraces many faiths.

All residents of the Virgin Islands who are citizens of the United States and 18 years of age or over have the right to vote in local elections. They do not send representatives to the U.S. Congress, nor do they participate in national elections. The people of the Virgin Islands have been citizens of the United States since 1927.

Tourism has become the main industry of the Virgin Islands. Tourist expenditures leaped from $4 million in 1951 to an estimated $200 million today. The pleasant year-round climate and the magnificent beaches, swimming, and snorkeling have made the Virgin Islands the prime tourist area of the Caribbean. Accommodations are plentiful and excellent. Jet travel has made the trip from the mainland convenient and relatively inexpensive. No passports or visas are necessary. The virtual free port status of the Islands and a special customs advantage of $200 in duty-free purchases are major attractions to shoppers. For this reason, the Islands have also become a popular port of call for cruise ships.

In addition to tourism, the Islands are attracting new industries to provide the broad base necessary for a stable economy. These include a new aluminum ore refining plant, an oil refinery, a knitting mill, and numerous factories. A tax incentive program is conducted to attract desirable new industries to the Islands. The making of rum continues as an important industry. Small truck farming is encouraged as is the raising of livestock. Water problems, caused in the past by unreliable rainfall and the small number of wells, are rapidly being solved through the conversion of salt water to fresh. Many other community improvement projects are helping to raise the local residents' standard of living.

Recalling Facts

1. Since 1960 the population of the Virgin Islands has
   □ a. increased.
   □ b. decreased.
   □ c. remained the same.

2. The three main languages of the Virgin Islands are
   □ a. English, Portuguese, and Dutch.
   □ b. English, French, and Spanish.
   □ c. English, German, and Welsh.

3. The people of the Virgin Islands have been United States citizens since
   □ a. 1900.
   □ b. 1927.
   □ c. 1942.

4. The principal industry of the Virgin Islands is
   □ a. manufacturing.
   □ b. tourism.
   □ c. agriculture.

5. A traveler may leave the Islands with duty-free purchases totaling
   □ a. $200.
   □ b. $400.
   □ c. $600.

Understanding the Passage

6. According to the author, residents of the Virgin Islands cannot
   □ a. vote in national elections.
   □ b. travel to other countries.
   □ c. use their money in the United States.

7. The author implies that the Virgin Islands were once owned by
   □ a. France.
   □ b. Denmark.
   □ c. Holland.

8. An American who visits the Virgin Islands
   □ a. must have a visa or a passport.
   □ b. can expect warm weather year-round.
   □ c. should carry a birth certificate.

9. Some of the drinking water in the Virgin Islands comes from
   □ a. community wells.
   □ b. converted sea water.
   □ c. large mountain reservoirs.

10. We can conclude that the
    □ a. economy of the Virgin Islands is expanding.
    □ b. Virgin Islands are popular with European vacationers.
    □ c. Virgin Islands are thought to be part of Atlantis.

14   Changes in the Landscape

Nature has made many billions of scars on the surface of the land through normal processes. Dry gulches, badlands, landfalls, alluvial washes, and terraces are among many landforms common to the geologist.

Meteor Crater in Arizona is a natural circular feature. It is attractive to many tourists, as is a large open pit near Bingham Canyon, Utah, created by people to recover billions of pounds of copper for industry. Roads and highways lace the country, as do streams in drainage basins. Lands are cleared for airports, transmission lines, railroads, and pipelines.

Some look upon any intrusion of the virgin wilderness to be a desecration of nature. The scientific advances that have set our life on earth apart from the rest of the animal world has indeed made a profound impact on the surface of this planet in many places. In order to sustain mankind on earth, landscape tradeoffs have been a necessary action. A growing population needs more natural resources each decade. Even if zero population growth is possible, mankind's demand for resources is staggering. Some estimate that total demand will double early in the year 2000.

The mature technical society of the United States has provided 50 to 100 times the wordly goods of its frontier counterpart. Today one penny's worth of gasoline provides the work of 25 people. Three people now provide the basic food for 100. Like it or not, this has been the accepted and preferred path of wealthy consumers and skillful technology.

Appalachia is scarred with remnants of open-pit coal mines that operated without any controls. For a fraction of the value of the coal marketed, most of these old sites might have been restored. Today the cost would reach hundreds of millions of dollars. On public lands in the western states, the Department of the Interior makes homeowners restore and reclaim land as part of the resource recovery mining system and part of the cost of operation. All leasing of public lands carries this important agreement.

A mature nation like the United States is dependent upon its natural resources. Thus, it cannot turn off its economic pattern of development without a major impact on its welfare and way of life. Nor can this nation continue its economic development without more concern for the environmental impact of its industry. This important issue requires the full attention and wisdom of government, and the concern of citizens.

*Reading Time*_____   *Comprehension Score*_____   *Words per Minute*_____

Recalling Facts

1. Meteor Crater is located in
   - ☐ a. California.
   - ☐ b. Nevada.
   - ☐ c. Arizona.

2. The author points out that landscape tradeoffs have been
   - ☐ a. disgraceful.
   - ☐ b. callous.
   - ☐ c. necessary.

3. Early in the year 2000, the need for natural resources may have
   - ☐ a. doubled.
   - ☐ b. tripled.
   - ☐ c. quadrupled.

4. Today one penny's worth of gasoline provides the work of
   - ☐ a. 10 horses.
   - ☐ b. 5 trucks.
   - ☐ c. 25 people.

5. Mining operations come under the authority of the Department of
   - ☐ a. Agriculture.
   - ☐ b. Commerce.
   - ☐ c. Interior.

Understanding the Passage

6. Meteor Crater is a
   - ☐ a. natural phenomenon.
   - ☐ b. scientific mystery.
   - ☐ c. man-made mining pit.

7. Appalachia is mentioned as an example of a
   - ☐ a. welfare district that needs more government money.
   - ☐ b. poverty area that has a high rate of crime.
   - ☐ c. mining region that has operated without controls.

8. The scarred remnants of the Appalachian mines serve as a warning against
   - ☐ a. the depletion of coal and other natural resources.
   - ☐ b. further advances of modern technology.
   - ☐ c. the irresponsible use of our natural resources.

9. The author develops these ideas through
   - ☐ a. mild criticism.
   - ☐ b. humorous commentary.
   - ☐ c. unkind sarcasm.

10. The author is in favor of
    - ☐ a. strong legislation prohibiting the use of our natural resources.
    - ☐ b. a better balance between economic growth and environmental protection.
    - ☐ c. continued economic development despite its impact on the environment.

15   The Imaginative Mr. Pearson

The key to successful forest fire fighting lies in speed of attack. "Hit 'em while they're small" has been the byword among Forest Service fire fighters since the organization was founded in 1905. Unless a forest fire is put out while it is still small, it can grow to alarming proportions with losses reaching millions of dollars.

Lightning is nature's own special fire starter. Each year, about 7,000 forest fires are caused by lightning throughout the Western United States. Many of these occur in remote, mountainous areas where helicopters cannot land and where ground travel is slow and difficult. Since the earliest days, foresters have searched for ways to speed the attack. Smoke jumping was born of this need.

The art and science of parachuting to fires is truly a Forest Service idea. The idea of parachuting firefighters to fires in distant areas was conceived in Utah in 1931 by an imaginative forester, T.V. Pearson. Pearson proposed and started the first experiments in the use of parachutes by forest fire fighters. He hired a professional parachutist to conduct demonstrations, but the idea was abandoned as being too risky.

For the next few years, the thought of parachuting firefighters to fires was only a glimmer in the minds of a few other foresters who had heard of Pearson's experiments.

In 1935, the United States Forest Service established an aerial fire control experimental project. The immediate plan was to experiment with air-dropped water and chemical bombs.

After several years of intensive experimentation to establish a good method of fire control from the air, it became apparent that control of fires with water or chemicals delivered by aircraft was impractical. The planes and equipment then available did not have the capability to deliver an effective blow to even the smallest forest fires.

David P. Godwin, assistant chief of fire control for the Forest Service, recommended that the bombing tests be discontinued and the balance of project funds be spent on a parachute jumping experiment. Parachutes, protective clothing, and the services of professional parachute riggers and jumpers were contracted. The experiment was conducted at Winthrop, Washington, during the fall of 1939. The tests showed that smoke jumpers could land safely in all kinds of green timber common to the Pacific Northwest at altitudes ranging from 2,000 to 6,800 feet above sea level. Jumps were also made in mountain meadows, open ridge tops, and on steep, boulder-strewn slopes.

Recalling Facts

1. The Forest Service fire
   fighters were organized in
   □ a. 1905.
   □ b. 1922.
   □ c. 1948.

2. The idea of parachuting
   firefighters into fire areas
   was conceived in
   □ a. Nebraska.
   □ b. North Carolina.
   □ c. Utah.

3. Smoke jumpers generally
   do not jump from planes
   lower than
   □ a. 500 feet.
   □ b. 1,000 feet.
   □ c. 2,000 feet.

4. How many fires are caused by
   lightning each year in the
   Western United States?
   □ a. 3,000
   □ b. 5,000
   □ c. 7,000

5. David P. Godwin worked for
   □ a. a parachute company.
   □ b. the Forest Service.
   □ c. a fire company.

Understanding the Passage

6. The idea of having planes drop water
   on fires was abandoned because
   □ a. airports were not located
       close enough to fires.
   □ b. pilots were afraid to fly into
       fire areas.
   □ c. planes could not carry enough
       water to be successful.

7. Parachuting tests were
   conducted in the
   □ a. New England area.
   □ b. Pacific Northwest.
   □ c. Southwest.

8. Smoke jumping has become a
   common method of fighting fires
   because
   □ a. some fires are inaccessible
       to vehicles.
   □ b. it is less expensive than conven-
       tional fire fighting methods.
   □ c. fire fighters like the challenge
       that aerial attack presents.

9. The article implies that the experiments of W. T. Pearson were
   □ a. widely published.
   □ b. kept a closely guarded secret.
   □ c. discussed in fire fighting
       circles.

10. We can conclude that
    □ a. smoke jumpers can control
        fires in all kinds of terrain.
    □ b. most fire fighters in forest
        areas are trained
        parachutists.
    □ c. experimentation with air-
        dropped water bombs is still
        conducted.

Every time a person eats something he makes a nutritional decision. He accepts or rejects the food available to him at home for meals or snacks. Or he selects food for himself at many places in the community, such as supermarkets, drive-ins, restaurants, and food counters in drugstores. These selections make a difference in how an individual looks, how he feels, and how well he can work and play.

When a good assortment of food in appropriate amounts is selected and eaten, the consequences are more likely to be a desirable level of health and enough energy to allow one to be as active as he needs and wants to be. When choices are less than desirable, the consequences are likely to be poor health or limited energy or both.

Studies of diets of individuals in the United States show that food selection is a highly individual matter, even among young children. Furthermore, far too many individuals of all ages are making poor choices day after day and are either now living with the consequences or will be in the future.

Nutritionists and workers in allied professions have been concerned about helping people learn to select and enjoy a wide variety of food combinations that can add up to a good diet.

Most people believe that they are well fed—that the choices they make are good ones. After all, they are not really sick, neither are they hungry. However, their nutrition is usually poor in one respect or another. Milk and milk products, such as cheeses, ice cream or milk, buttermilk, and yogurt, are often slighted. Then people may skip many fruits and vegetables, particularly those that are good sources of vitamins A and C. These include dark green, leafy vegetables; deep yellow vegetables; and citrus fruits and vegetables, such as cabbage, tomatoes, and green peppers.

Every American has the right to choose to be uninformed about nutrition as well as to be informed. If a person believes that she is well fed, attitudes, habits, and information cannot be forced upon her.

There are life situations, however, that tend to cause an individual to want to know how to make the best choices. For example, a young person setting up her own apartment is for the first time completely responsible for the household food supply. Or perhaps a young couple is starting a family and must prepare food for young children.

Recalling Facts

1. Green leafy vegetables contain large amounts of
   ☐ a. vitamin C.
   ☐ b. vitamin D.
   ☐ c. vitamin E.

2. Food preference in America is
   ☐ a. culturally oriented.
   ☐ b. inherited.
   ☐ c. individualistic.

3. People often overlook the nutritional value of
   ☐ a. ice cream.
   ☐ b. cereal.
   ☐ c. bread.

4. Good amounts of vitamin A can be found in
   ☐ a. celery.
   ☐ b. bananas.
   ☐ c. cabbage.

5. The article points out that nutrition is related to
   ☐ a. aging.
   ☐ b. energy.
   ☐ c. reproduction.

Understanding the Passage

6. According to the author, nutritionists are concerned with
   ☐ a. improving the vitamin content of processed foods.
   ☐ b. restricting the manufacture of high cholesterol foods.
   ☐ c. informing the public about wholesome foods.

7. The author implies that many Americans are
   ☐ a. overweight.
   ☐ b. vitamin conscious.
   ☐ c. poorly nourished.

8. Some people judge their nutrition by the
   ☐ a. status of their health.
   ☐ b. grocery stores where they shop.
   ☐ c. amount of protein in their diets.

9. From the information provided, we can assume that
   ☐ a. dietary deficiencies become apparent many years later.
   ☐ b. animal fats often cause high cholesterol levels in the blood.
   ☐ c. many people do not consume enough sugar.

10. The author advocates
    ☐ a. requiring high school students to take courses on nutrition.
    ☐ b. making information on nutrition available to the public.
    ☐ c. forcing food manufacturers to list ingredients on packages.

17 Paying for Protection

When purchasing life insurance, there are many important factors to consider. One should buy the policies that give the most protection at the least cost, insure the right family members, and consider the family's financial needs. It is important to buy the insurance from companies that are financially sound and that are represented by honest, well-trained agents.

At various stages in a person's life different kinds of life insurance are needed for particular situations.

Jerry is single and has no dependents. Probably the only life insurance he needs is enough to cover his debts and burial expenses. Insurance can be purchased at a lower rate during the young years, but, by buying while young, the premiums are paid for a longer period of time. In the end, the amount paid in for premiums is about the same. A person shouldn't buy insurance protection that really isn't necessary.

Suppose that Jerry marries Jeannette, who is a college graduate and is working. Perhaps enough insurance would be needed to cover their debts and burial expenses.

Later, Jeannette has quit work and their first child is on the way. They have purchased a home with a small down payment and a thirty-year mortgage. The situation regarding life insurance takes on a different look. There are dependents who need financial protection. How much insurance is needed?

As the family increases in size, it is essential to add more insurance on the breadwinner to protect the dependents. When the children are young and depend upon the family for financial needs, families with modest incomes have difficulties providing enough life insurance to protect the mother and the children.

Families with modest incomes should insure the breadwinner or breadwinners first. When considering the amount of insurance for the mother with dependent children, substitute child care is a need that should be planned for until the children can care for themselves. The death of a small child would have no effect upon the income of the family. Perhaps a policy to meet funeral expenses would be sufficient for the young child, although most people do not take out insurance on their young children.

As the children become financially independent of the family, the emphasis on family financial security will shift from protection to saving for the retirement years. Every family situation is different. But it is important that each family give adequate thought and study to planning its financial future.

Recalling Facts

1. When the article first mentions Jerry, he is
   - ☐ a. single.
   - ☐ b. married.
   - ☐ c. divorced.

2. Insurance that is purchased when a person is young is
   - ☐ a. a poor investment.
   - ☐ b. an inexpensive investment.
   - ☐ c. a risky investment.

3. In the article, Jeannette is
   - ☐ a. educated.
   - ☐ b. insecure.
   - ☐ c. sickly.

4. Jerry and Jeannette buy a house with a mortgage lasting
   - ☐ a. 20 years.
   - ☐ b. 25 years.
   - ☐ c. 30 years.

5. As children are born, insurance should be increased on the
   - ☐ a. older children.
   - ☐ b. breadwinner.
   - ☐ c. home.

Understanding the Passage

6. The author implies that
   - ☐ a. insurance rates are different with each company.
   - ☐ b. children should be insured against illnesses.
   - ☐ c. funeral expenses are not as great as most people think.

7. As a person's responsibilities increase, he or she should
   - ☐ a. make insurance payments ahead of time.
   - ☐ b. consider rewriting his or her will.
   - ☐ c. expand his or her insurance coverage.

8. We can infer from the article that a major aim of life insurance is to
   - ☐ a. provide for the sudden loss of family income.
   - ☐ b. enhance the family's yearly income.
   - ☐ c. accumulate funds for future retirement.

9. The author implies that life insurance may change when
   - ☐ a. a family moves.
   - ☐ b. a person changes jobs.
   - ☐ c. children leave home.

10. The most reliable insurance companies
    - ☐ a. are represented by well-trained agents.
    - ☐ b. offer all types of insurance.
    - ☐ c. have branch offices in many cities.

18 Trees on Our Streets

The best trees for any area of the country are those, either native or exotic, able to thrive under the area's prevailing climatic conditions. In wide-ranging species like the red maple or the red oak, it is best to select from northern populations for cold hardiness.

Trees that are borderline cases are not worth the time and money. For instance, the lovely streets of live oaks in Alabama cannot be duplicated in Washington, D.C., even if seedlings from the northernmost outpost of that species in Virginia are used.

Even when trees have climatic survival potential, however, the variability among seedlings argues against their use in city planting.

We demand much from our city trees. We want uniform and high survival. After all, the young trees planted on our streets cost more than a mature tree of the same species is worth as timber. We want uniform and maximum resistance to pests and to urban stress factors. We usually want uniformity of growth rate and tree form for aesthetic reasons. The only way to achieve these goals is clonal selection.

A clone is a group of plants derived asexually from a single individual. The members of a clone are reproduced from the original tree through grafting, budding, or the rooting of cuttings and are all genetically identical. In current horticultural practice selected clones are called "cultivars" and they are given fancy names. The Bradford pear, selected and introduced by the United States Department of Agriculture, is an example of a new and useful shade tree cultivar.

The clone or cultivar thus gives us the maximum in uniformity for desirable characteristics. The clone is also uniform in undesirable traits. If, for example, a well-shaped, fast-growing clone of honeylocust has not been tested and selected for resistance to the mimosa webworm, the steady spread of this introduced insect pest might decimate large-scale plantings of this clone and make chemical spraying the only chance for survival.

There are many cultivars of shade trees currently in the nursery trade—maples, ashes, lindens, and others. But almost without exception, these cultivars have been selected only for their growth and form characteristics. Their resistance or susceptibility to major insect and disease pests is unknown. Their tolerance of urban stress factors such as air pollution and salt is likewise undetermined. The only way to select the best possible trees is through an adequate testing program.

Recalling Facts

1. A clone is produced by
   - ☐ a. cross-pollination.
   - ☐ b. grafting.
   - ☐ c. root trimming.

2. The Bradford pear is mentioned as an excellent tree for
   - ☐ a. color.
   - ☐ b. fruit.
   - ☐ c. shade.

3. Honeylocust is often affected by
   - ☐ a. worms.
   - ☐ b. cold temperatures.
   - ☐ c. leaf wilt.

4. Cultivars are usually selected for their
   - ☐ a. shape.
   - ☐ b. disease resistance.
   - ☐ c. colorful blossoms.

5. A cultivar that can be purchased in nurseries is
   - ☐ a. a maple.
   - ☐ b. a dogwood.
   - ☐ c. an elm.

Understanding the Passage

6. The author implies that red oaks
   - ☐ a. are common in many areas.
   - ☐ b. grow best in warm climates.
   - ☐ c. will not grow in the North.

7. According to the author, a cultivar is
   - ☐ a. more difficult to breed than a clone.
   - ☐ b. less expensive than a clone.
   - ☐ c. the same as a clone.

8. In order to produce a clone,
   - ☐ a. a male and a female tree must grow near each other.
   - ☐ b. a group of trees from one climate must be used.
   - ☐ c. only one tree of superior quality is used.

9. According to the article, a clone inherits from the parent tree
   - ☐ a. only desirable traits.
   - ☐ b. identical traits, good or bad.
   - ☐ c. mostly undesirable traits.

10. The reader can infer that
    - ☐ a. all forms of oak trees survive well in the North.
    - ☐ b. clonal selection is a relatively new method of tree production.
    - ☐ c. urban trees are very susceptible to drought.

An ocean-going research vessel is heading for the lobster grounds off Boothbay Harbor, Maine. A team of diver-biologists is putting on the latest in scuba equipment.

When the vessel reaches the fishing grounds, the anchor is set and the team enters the water.

At 90 feet below surface, the divers find lobsters. Experimental work begins. Through firsthand observations the divers record the way in which lobsters live, how they behave, feed, and move about.

Of what importance is such research? One goal is to determine the number of lobsters that can be caught without overfishing. Overfishing would reduce the number that can be caught in future years. Another goal is to determine whether present fishing methods can be improved. Forward-looking biologists are also dealing with the possibility of raising lobsters artificially. If this is to be done, the conditions under which lobsters can be cultivated must be determined. What better way is there to do this than to make scientific observations directly on the lobster and its environment?

Three thousand miles away, along the southern California coast, another team of diver-biologists is preparing to enter the compression chamber that will carry them below surface waters to a depth of 450 feet. There the chamber, which has been slowly pressurized to the water pressure at this depth, is opened. The team swims a short distance to enter the already-anchored Sealab III.

The divers will live in this underwater dwelling for two weeks with their lungs filled with a mixture of helium and oxygen. Since the pressure in their bodies and living quarters is the same as that of the surrounding water, the divers will be able to leave and enter Sealab III at will. In this way they will be able to conduct research that will tell more about marine life and how it can be used to the advantage of mankind.

Marine scientists have also been working with our space scientists. Astronauts have taken photographs of certain coastal and oceanic areas around the globe. This is called spacecraft oceanography. It tells us where areas of abundance of fish and shellfish might be expected, and where the waters would yield nothing to the fisherman.

These are but a few of the many exciting new techniques that are being explored and developed by scientists. They help us to understand the nature of the ocean and the living aquatic resources it contains.

Recalling Facts

1. What two states are mentioned in the article?
   - ☐ a. Alaska and Florida
   - ☐ b. Mississippi and Oregon
   - ☐ c. Maine and California

2. Lobsters are often found at depths of
   - ☐ a. 90 feet.
   - ☐ b. 150 feet.
   - ☐ c. 220 feet.

3. Sealab III can operate at a depth of
   - ☐ a. 450 feet.
   - ☐ b. 1,000 feet.
   - ☐ c. 1,600 feet.

4. Divers remain in Sealab III for periods of
   - ☐ a. one week.
   - ☐ b. two weeks.
   - ☐ c. three weeks.

5. The atmosphere in Sealab III is composed of oxygen and
   - ☐ a. helium.
   - ☐ b. nitrogen.
   - ☐ c. neon.

Understanding the Passage

6. One goal of oceanographic research is to
   - ☐ a. find precious minerals beneath the sea.
   - ☐ b. explore the nature of marine life.
   - ☐ c. study methods of reducing pollution.

7. The purpose of spacecraft oceanography is to locate
   - ☐ a. oil spills and trace their progress.
   - ☐ b. schools of migrating fish.
   - ☐ c. productive fishing areas.

8. The author implies that scientists are concerned with the
   - ☐ a. extinction of lobsters.
   - ☐ b. reproductive patterns of whales.
   - ☐ c. relationship between survival and intelligence.

9. The article states that marine life is studied
   - ☐ a. through the use of delicate underwater instruments.
   - ☐ b. from permanent underwater stations.
   - ☐ c. through personal observations.

10. We can conclude that
    - ☐ a. some forms of shellfish may be grown artificially in the future.
    - ☐ b. most countries have established a 200-mile fishing limit.
    - ☐ c. courses in oceanography are offered at many universities.

The first step in starting a new dry cleaning business is to determine the market that the store will serve. The future businessperson must identify the general type of consumer. For example, the person may wish to cater to lower income inner-city residents or to the residents of a suburban area with a particular income and ethnic character.

Whatever the decision, it will affect the location, the size, and the services of the store. In lower income areas, for example, a wide range of services is not needed. Prices must be lower than standard, and profit must come through large volume and maximum efficiency.

The general procedure to be followed in choosing a store location begins with the identification of several potential locations where space is available. Next, the businessperson must compute the number of potential customers within the area of each location, and determine the amount of monthly expenditures each customer will make on dry cleaning. An analysis of competition in each area will also show where new markets are needed.

A number of cities have organizations that specialize in assisting minority businesspeople to secure capital. A prospective entrepreneur should seek out these sources and go over any plans with them.

The local Small Business Administration office or Office of Minority Business Enterprise affiliate may help put the businessperson in touch with sources of capital and provide the names of banks that have made loans to minority individuals. Minority-owned banks may also be sources of debt financing.

The Small Business Administration can also help with a lease guarantee. Many landlords are unwilling to lease to a new and inexperienced businessperson because they have no recourse in the event the business fails. The SBA has a program to reassure such landlords by insuring the lease of the small businessperson.

There are many legal details that must be attended to before starting a business. The prospective entrepreneur must get a license or permit to do business and will probably need to have a boiler permit as well. The entrepreneur must find out these requirements before starting operations.

Insurance is also a major factor to be considered. Basic insurance includes fire, theft, and vandalism coverage. Because the dry cleaner is responsible for customers' costly garments while they are entrusted to his care, bailee insurance is a requirement. Also, since customers, salespeople, and visitors enter the store, public liability protection is important.

Recalling Facts

1. The Small Business Administration can provide
   - ☐ a. purchase money.
   - ☐ b. lease guarantees.
   - ☐ c. new customers.

2. The small business mentioned in the article is a
   - ☐ a. dry cleaning store.
   - ☐ b. grocery store.
   - ☐ c. record shop.

3. A person is most likely to find the Small Business Administration in
   - ☐ a. large cities.
   - ☐ b. small towns.
   - ☐ c. rural areas.

4. The amount of money each customer will spend is figured on a
   - ☐ a. daily basis.
   - ☐ b. weekly basis.
   - ☐ c. monthly basis.

5. The Small Business Administration can introduce businesspeople to
   - ☐ a. banks.
   - ☐ b. customers.
   - ☐ c. landlords.

Understanding the Passage

6. According to the author the first step in starting a small business is
   - ☐ a. buying a large store.
   - ☐ b. finding a reliable wholesaler.
   - ☐ c. understanding the customer.

7. In low income areas, stores must
   - ☐ a. offer a wide range of services.
   - ☐ b. sell on a small volume basis.
   - ☐ c. sell items and services at low cost.

8. The author's tone may be described as
   - ☐ a. amusing.
   - ☐ b. informative.
   - ☐ c. emotional.

9. The author implies that the Small Business Administration
   - ☐ a. is a self-supporting agency.
   - ☐ b. provides important assistance.
   - ☐ c. oversimplifies business problems.

10. We may conclude that starting a small business
   - ☐ a. is a dangerous and costly process.
   - ☐ b. involves many government agencies.
   - ☐ c. requires much advanced planning.

Thomas Jefferson has been called "America's Architect," not because he built one of the most revolutionary houses of his day, but because he designed and wrote the most important revolutionary document of the modern age. In a time when revolution was commonplace in America, Jefferson was asked to write the Declaration of Independence, the ageless announcement of colonial freedom.

Deprived of his father at the age of 14, Jefferson inherited "Little Mountain," which he renamed in Italian, "Monticello." He began building his dream house at the age of 20 and finally finished it forty years later in the twilight of his life. Monticello, pictured in careful detail on the back of the nickel, is not an ordinary house. Built on top of Carter's Mountain, Monticello has an observatory where Jefferson studied the stars and planets with a telescope. The clock in the house's main hall not only tells the hour, but the days of the week as well. The gears that drive the hands of the clock pass through the wall to a duplicate clock over the porch outside. The house has dozens of other amazing conveniences. Jefferson was a gadgeteer, a man of creative genius who put his ideas to practical use.

Jefferson was an amazing man. Being a true architect, he designed and built the University of Virginia campus, the capitol building of Richmond, and several of his neighbors' homes. He was also an inventor, a lawyer, a violinist, a statesman, and served as the President of the United States.

Despite the fact that he had many talents, he is best remembered as a defender of man's human rights. Jefferson wrote the Declaration of Independence and the Virginia Statute for Religious Freedom. He served in the Continental Congress, in President Washington's cabinet, and as a United States foreign minister. He spoke to the world through his pen. He preferred to put his thoughts in writing rather than in public speech. For this reason, he has often been referred to as the silent member of the Congress.

Devoted to a personal dream of an empire of liberty for the American nation, Jefferson believed, with all his heart, in the future of the United States of America. His attempts to assure liberty for all men were summed up in the statement, "I have sworn upon the altar of God, eternal hostility against every form of tyranny over the mind of man."

Recalling Facts

1. According to the author, "Monticello" means
   - ☐ a. shining waters.
   - ☐ b. quiet place.
   - ☐ c. little mountain.

2. Jefferson's home is pictured on the back of the
   - ☐ a. dime.
   - ☐ b. nickel.
   - ☐ c. penny.

3. Jefferson played the
   - ☐ a. flute.
   - ☐ b. piano.
   - ☐ c. violin.

4. Jefferson began to build Monticello when he was
   - ☐ a. 20 years old.
   - ☐ b. 35 years old.
   - ☐ c. 50 years old.

5. The author states that Jefferson was
   - ☐ a. an inventor.
   - ☐ b. a general.
   - ☐ c. a governor.

Understanding the Passage

6. At the time that the *Declaration of Independence* was written,
   - ☐ a. Jefferson was working as a lawyer in Virginia.
   - ☐ b. most colonies were in favor of breaking away from England.
   - ☐ c. people had little faith in America.

7. Jefferson felt that tyranny was the
   - ☐ a. enemy of freedom.
   - ☐ b. altar of God.
   - ☐ c. only way to control the masses.

8. Jefferson is best remembered as
   - ☐ a. America's third president.
   - ☐ b. a great foreign diplomat.
   - ☐ c. a defender of human rights.

9. The title of this article, "America's Architect," refers to Jefferson's
   - ☐ a. genius in home designs.
   - ☐ b. work on the *Declaration of Independence*.
   - ☐ c. dream of unity between the North and the South.

10. The design of Monticello shows that Jefferson
    - ☐ a. was a clever person.
    - ☐ b. cared about people's happiness.
    - ☐ c. followed English customs.

22 Cancer

Each of the billions of cells that make up your body has a special job. Skin cells give protection. Red blood cells carry oxygen. And bone cells build the skeleton. These cells multiply rapidly during childhood, but once you reach maturity, they divide and reproduce themselves only to replace worn-out tissues or to repair wounds. Cancer cells seem to be runaway cells that multiply rapidly and without purpose. The cancer growth takes food needed by the normal cells. It invades healthy tissues and spreads to other parts of the body. The patient can be cured only by removal or destruction of all cancer cells.

It is widely believed that parents do not pass cancer on to their children, but doctors sometimes find that two or more members of a family may develop the same type of cancer.

Medical science still does not know how the change from a normal to an abnormal cell takes place. Research, however, has produced new information about the causes of some forms of cancer. Cigarette smoking has been cited as the major cause of lung cancer. Other cancer hazards include repeated or prolonged exposure to sunlight or to X-rays, to the fumes of certain industrial chemicals, and perhaps to polluted air.

Cancer appears most often in men and women over 35, but younger people and sometimes even babies are affected. Science knows three ways to arrest and, in some instances, cure cancer. Surgery removes cancer growths and nearby tissues that may contain cancer cells. Radiation from X-rays and radioactive elements destroys cancer cells. Chemotherapy, or treatment with drugs, sometimes completely, though temporarily, relieves symptoms and shrinks tumors when other types of treatment do not work well. Research in combinations of these three methods is always going on in an effort to increase the effectiveness of treatment. Safer, more effective surgery, improved methods of radiation, and better use of drugs improve the outlook for cancer patients. Because methods of detection have improved, cancer is often discovered in an early, localized stage when treatment may help.

You can protect yourself and your family by knowing the danger signs of cancer and reporting any of these to your doctor at once. Every person should have a complete physical exam at least once a year. You can avoid those habits known to lead to some forms of cancer. You can guard against such health hazards as air and water pollution.

Recalling Facts

1. The author calls cancer cells
   - ☐ a. evil growths.
   - ☐ b. immature cells.
   - ☐ c. runaway cells.

2. Doctors believe that one form of cancer may be caused by
   - ☐ a. poor nutrition.
   - ☐ b. polluted air.
   - ☐ c. inadequate housing.

3. Cancer appears most frequently in men and women over
   - ☐ a. 25.
   - ☐ b. 35.
   - ☐ c. 45.

4. Chemotherapy is a form of treatment that uses
   - ☐ a. radiation.
   - ☐ b. surgery.
   - ☐ c. drugs.

5. Every person should have a physical examination every
   - ☐ a. six months.
   - ☐ b. year.
   - ☐ c. two years.

Understanding the Passage

6. Doctors sometimes find that
   - ☐ a. two brothers may develop the same form of cancer.
   - ☐ b. cancer cells result from a previous injury.
   - ☐ c. radiation increases the risk of cancer.

7. The article points out that
   - ☐ a. most cancers seem to be inherited.
   - ☐ b. scientists are puzzled by cell changes.
   - ☐ c. cells continue to multiply rapidly after childhood.

8. The purpose of this article is to
   - ☐ a. give a general overview of cancer.
   - ☐ b. discuss specific research now being conducted.
   - ☐ c. illustrate surgery techniques of several cancer forms.

9. The author does not discuss
   - ☐ a. symptoms of cancer.
   - ☐ b. causes of cancer.
   - ☐ c. protection against cancer.

10. We can conclude that
   - ☐ a. all body cells have the potential for cancer.
   - ☐ b. more money than ever is being spent on cancer research.
   - ☐ c. surgery is the most common method of eliminating cancer.

Farmington, Utah, is a more pleasant community since a local girls 4-H Club improved Main Street. Six 4-H girls worked to clean a 72-foot curbside that was covered with weeds, rocks, and litter. Each member volunteered to clean up and to dig and plant five flats of Comanche petunias. They also took turns in watering, weeding, and maintaining the plot.

Participation in this project helped the girls develop a new attitude toward the appearance of their own homes. They have learned how to work with tools and have improved their work habits. One mother said that before her daughter was involved in this project, she would not even pull a weed. The experience on Main Street stimulated self-improvement and encouraged members to take pride in their home grounds and in the total community.

A few years ago, a violent storm caused a group of young people to act in Yamhill County, Oregon. The Baker Creek 4-H Club of McMinnville pledged its support to help restore the beauty of Edward Grenfell Park. This county park became a community improvement project with adults and young people teaming up to reclaim the recreational area.

County officials cooperated with the 4-H members in planting trees and shrubs, building cooking facilities, picnic tables, swings, and comfort stations. The 4-H'ers planted hemlock and western red cedar trees as seedlings and nurtured them during the early stages of growth. The total park project needed more plantings in the following years. Members of the Baker Creek 4-H Club agreed to follow the project through to completion because they received satisfaction from the results of constructive work.

Teamwork was needed for a beautification project in Indiantown, Florida. The two 4-H Clubs and the Kiwanis Club in this small community began a program to develop a central recreational facility. The need for a facility was recognized by the leading industrial firm in the community. The firm made available a large block of land in the center of town for a community park and recreational area. Under direction of the county commissioner, the 4-H members planted a portion of the park, and the Kiwanis Club provided a palm-thatched picnic shelter and large picnic tables.

The project is a growing one and has spread from the park to the school and the shopping center. Palms, flowers, and shrubbery have all been planted in the shopping center, making the atmosphere pleasant.

Recalling Facts

1. One group of 4-H members planted
   - ☐ a. geraniums.
   - ☐ b. tulips.
   - ☐ c. petunias.

2. Yamhill County is located in the state of
   - ☐ a. Washington.
   - ☐ b. Oregon.
   - ☐ c. Virginia.

3. An organization that has helped 4-H groups is the
   - ☐ a. Kiwanis Club.
   - ☐ b. Lions Club.
   - ☐ c. Knights of Columbus.

4. The 4-H work cited in the article benefited
   - ☐ a. large cities.
   - ☐ b. rural areas.
   - ☐ c. small towns.

5. One 4-H group was motivated to beautify a park because of
   - ☐ a. a large donation.
   - ☐ b. a storm.
   - ☐ c. new leadership.

Understanding the Passage

6. One mother indicated that before her daughter became involved, she
   - ☐ a. received low grades in school.
   - ☐ b. refused to care for her younger brothers.
   - ☐ c. lacked ambition to work around the home.

7. This article is primarily about
   - ☐ a. cooperation among city officials.
   - ☐ b. the specialized work of some community groups.
   - ☐ c. the efforts of youth groups to end pollution.

8. One industrial firm mentioned in the article was
   - ☐ a. insensitive to the needs of the community.
   - ☐ b. generous with its donations to several charities.
   - ☐ c. eager to provide a recreational area for the community.

9. Some 4-H members working on various projects have
   - ☐ a. learned how to use tools.
   - ☐ b. discovered the joys of helping the less fortunate.
   - ☐ c. influenced large corporations to donate money regularly.

10. The reader can conclude that
    - ☐ a. participation in community projects is a maturing experience.
    - ☐ b. 4-H leaders usually volunteer their services.
    - ☐ c. most charitable work is done without public recognition.

Drug addiction is the physical dependence upon a drug. Its definition includes the development of tolerance and withdrawal. As a person develops tolerance, he requires larger and larger amounts of the drug to achieve the same effect. Withdrawal occurs when the use of an addicting drug is stopped. It is characterized by a wide range of distressing symptoms such as diarrhea, vomiting, and cramps. Many drug users develop a compulsion to continue taking a drug to avoid the withdrawal symptoms.

Many people think drugs are magic potions that have only good effects. However, almost every drug is potentially dangerous at some dosage level for certain people under some circumstances. Some drugs can also be harmful when taken in dangerous combinations or by very sensitive people in small or ordinary amounts.

The fact that some drugs can bring about beneficial results does not mean that pills will solve all problems. What is needed is a new respect for all drugs. Drugs that affect the mind can have subtle or obvious effects, which may occur immediately or become evident only after long-term, continuous use.

All drugs have many effects that vary among individuals, on different occasions in the same individual, with the amount of the drug and the length of time the drug is used. Many factors not related to the chemical makeup of the drug cause varying effects. These include the expectations of the user, the circumstances under which he takes the drug, and the meaning of drug use to the individual.

Even the same individual taking the same dose of a drug on subsequent occasions may have a completely different reaction. As the drug affects the individual, he becomes more susceptible to the moods of the people around him and affected by his surroundings. These factors can markedly alter the drug's effects on an individual.

A user can ask his family, friend, physician, or minister to help him find the best resource in the community. The family doctor, mental health professionals, or school counselors should be among the first contacted. Some community mental health centers have special drug abuse units; all centers can provide referral to appropriate resources.

The harmful, and the beneficial uses of drugs should be understood. Children should not be continually exposed to the idea that the stresses of daily life require chemical relief. Respect for all chemicals, especially mind-altering chemicals, should be instilled in children at an early age.

Recalling Facts

1. Vomiting, cramps, and diarrhea are symptoms of
   - ☐ a. addiction.
   - ☐ b. overdose.
   - ☐ c. withdrawal.

2. Many people think of a drug as a
   - ☐ a. magic potion.
   - ☐ b. pleasant escape.
   - ☐ c. necessary medicine.

3. The article points out that drugs can be harmful if taken
   - ☐ a. in combinations.
   - ☐ b. in pill form.
   - ☐ c. without prescription.

4. The author says that children should not be continually exposed to
   - ☐ a. the stresses of life.
   - ☐ b. maltreatment.
   - ☐ c. the need for medicine.

5. Drug addition is considered a
   - ☐ a. mental dependence.
   - ☐ b. physical dependence.
   - ☐ c. social dependence.

Understanding the Passage

6. The author implies that
   - ☐ a. tolerance levels are different for each person.
   - ☐ b. teenagers take drugs because of social pressure.
   - ☐ c. drugs often cause serious side effects in the elderly.

7. The author advises the reader to
   - ☐ a. study medicine labels carefully.
   - ☐ b. use drugs cautiously.
   - ☐ c. have a physical examination yearly.

8. The author suggests that
   - ☐ a. only a few drugs can be dangerous.
   - ☐ b. drugs lose their potency as they age.
   - ☐ c. drugs work at varying speeds.

9. The author feels that the most dangerous drugs
   - ☐ a. can cause vitamin deficiencies.
   - ☐ b. affect the mind.
   - ☐ c. enlarge the liver.

10. The article leads the reader to believe that
    - ☐ a. a person's attitude can modify the effects of a drug.
    - ☐ b. drugs are always harmful in large doses.
    - ☐ c. organic compounds are safer than drugs.

25　A Long-suppressed Hatred

For hundreds of years before the Spanish colonized the southwest, Indians had lived along the Rio Grande in what is now New Mexico. They were good farmers, made pretty pottery, and wove fine cotton cloth. Above all, they were very religious. The supernatural influenced everything they did.

In 1598, colonists and priests from Mexico under Don Juan de Onate set up among these Indians the first Spanish community in the Southwest. The new settlers called the Indians "Pueblos" because of the Indians' remarkable villages of large timber and adobe houses. Onate, the new settlement's governor, had Catholic missions and churches built. And, in 1610, he established a territorial capital at Santa Fe.

The Pueblos' ancient way of life was soon threatened. Considered subjects of the Spanish crown, Indians were required to pay taxes in the form of cloth, corn, or labor. Their villages were renamed after Catholic saints, and their own ceremonies and religious practices were forbidden.

In 1675, a leader arose among the Pueblo Indians in the person of Pope, a medicine man. Pope had been imprisoned by the Spanish under suspicion of witchcraft and the killing of several missionaries. He bitterly hated the white occupiers. Released from prison, he went into hiding and planned an all-Pueblo rebellion. He intended to bring back the Indians' old beliefs and customs. Runners secretly carried this message to all the Pueblos, and native towns eagerly joined the plot. Every precaution was taken to keep the Spanish from learning of the conspiracy.

August 13, 1680, was the date set for the attack. Somehow, however, the news leaked out, and Pope's only hope was to strike at once. On August 10, with the force of a long-suppressed hatred, the Indians attacked.

Nearly 500 of the 2,500 Spanish people were killed. About 30 priests were murdered in their missions, their bodies stacked upon the altars. Santa Fe, the Spanish capital, was attacked, and its 1,000 inhabitants took refuge in official buildings for about ten days. Then, after forcing the Indians to a temporary retreat, they fled from Santa Fe.

Having driven out the occupiers, the triumphant Pope then set out to erase all traces of them. Indians who had been baptized as Christians were washed with yucca suds, and use of the Spanish language and all baptismal names was prohibited. Pope did all he could to restore the old Pueblo way of life.

Recalling Facts

1. The achievements of the Pueblos were influenced by their
   - ☐ a. superstitions.
   - ☐ b. Bible.
   - ☐ c. elders.

2. The first Spanish settlement was established in the late
   - ☐ a. 1540s.
   - ☐ b. 1590s.
   - ☐ c. 1630s.

3. The Pueblos were so named because of their
   - ☐ a. farming techniques.
   - ☐ b. hostile nature.
   - ☐ c. building materials.

4. Before Pope organized a plot to drive out the whites, he was a
   - ☐ a. teacher.
   - ☐ b. medicine man.
   - ☐ c. chief.

5. The outcome of the battle for Santa Fe was
   - ☐ a. an Indian victory.
   - ☐ b. a Spanish victory.
   - ☐ c. a draw.

Understanding the Passage

6. Don Juan de Onate forced the Indians to
   - ☐ a. learn how to read and write.
   - ☐ b. adopt the Catholic faith.
   - ☐ c. return to Mexico.

7. Pope's attack on Santa Fe
   - ☐ a. was delayed for several days.
   - ☐ b. occurred ahead of schedule.
   - ☐ c. was launched without planning.

8. After the battle for Santa Fe, Pope
   - ☐ a. returned to Mexico and planned a new attack.
   - ☐ b. reinstated Indian culture.
   - ☐ c. established friendly relations with the Spanish.

9. Indians were forced to pay taxes with
   - ☐ a. small pieces of gold from local streams.
   - ☐ b. money from the sale of handicrafts.
   - ☐ c. crops from their own land.

10. We can conclude that
    - ☐ a. the Indians were not respected as intelligent beings.
    - ☐ b. primitive cultures cannot develop without help.
    - ☐ c. Spanish customs are closely related to Indian customs.

A cancer-causing factor in our environment is the light of the sun. The ultraviolet radiation story begins in Germany in 1894, when scientists expressed their belief that too much exposure to sunlight was related to skin cancer. In 1928, English scientists succeeded in producing skin cancer in experimental animals exposed to bright sunlight.

The cancer-producing effects of the ultraviolet rays of sunlight seem to be limited to the skin. It has been noticed that the incidence of skin cancer is highest in the southern and western parts of the United States and lowest in the North. Furthermore, skin cancer occurs more often among people who work outdoors, such as sailors and farmers, than among people who can guard themselves against too much exposure to the sun.

The color of the skin is another factor. Cancer of the skin is most common among fair-skinned people. It is much less common among black people and others with dark skin.

Related to the cancer-causing effects of sunlight is the discovery of the dangers of ionizing radiation from radium and X-rays. This discovery was actually made on human beings. Early radiologists developed dryness, ulcers, and eventually, cancer of their hands. In 1910, a French worker produced skin cancer in a rat following application of radium to the skin.

Ionizing radiation can cause several forms of cancer in man and in animals. Radiologists and others exposed to increased doses of radiation are more likely to develop leukemia than are people who are not so exposed. The people of Hiroshima and Nagasaki who lived through the exposure to atomic bombs have been studied carefully by scientists. Information obtained in the course of their investigations leaves no doubt that a single radiation exposure at high doses can produce leukemia in humans.

Radium salts, which have been found to build up in bone, give rise to cancers of the bone. A historical tragedy was the deaths from bone cancer of factory women who pointed with their lips the brushes they used in painting watch dials with radium.

Man-made sources of ionizing radiation are definitely one of the more serious possible cancer-producing hazards. One of the key issues involved is the question of dose. Does a radiation dose have to reach some specific level before becoming dangerous, or does any amount of radiation increase one's risk to cancer? This problem, of course, also exists in considering cancer-causing chemicals.

Recalling Facts

1. Which person is most likely to
   develop skin cancer?
   - ☐ a. an athlete
   - ☐ b. a secretary
   - ☐ c. a farmer

2. Skin cancer is caused by
   - ☐ a. gamma rays.
   - ☐ b. ultraviolet rays.
   - ☐ c. alpha rays.

3. Cancer of the skin is most
   common among people
   who have
   - ☐ a. fair complexions.
   - ☐ b. dark hair.
   - ☐ c. blue eyes.

4. Ionizing radiation is
   produced by
   - ☐ a. ulcers.
   - ☐ b. radium.
   - ☐ c. charged electrons.

5. The people of Hiroshima have
   been studied for symptoms of
   - ☐ a. skin cancer.
   - ☐ b. leukemia.
   - ☐ c. bone cancer.

Understanding the Passage

6. The author mentions factory
   women who died of cancer
   because they
   - ☐ a. inhaled large amounts of
     asbestos fiber.
   - ☐ b. consumed small amounts
     of radium.
   - ☐ c. were exposed to X-rays.

7. According to the author,
   radium salts
   - ☐ a. can cure some cases of
     bone cancer.
   - ☐ b. accumulate in bone
     structures.
   - ☐ c. cause bones to become
     brittle.

8. Research on ultraviolet radiation
   began
   - ☐ a. less than twenty-five
     years ago.
   - ☐ b. about fifty years ago.
   - ☐ c. about one hundred years ago.

9. Most of the early research on
   cancer was conducted in
   - ☐ a. European countries.
   - ☐ b. the United States.
   - ☐ c. Japan.

10. Scientists have not yet determined
    - ☐ a. the level at which radiation
      becomes dangerous.
    - ☐ b. the danger of man-made
      radiation.
    - ☐ c. which occupations involve
      the greater cancer risk.

27 The Ocean at Work

If people are to live and build along coasts and out into the sea, they will need to understand and to predict marine geological processes. Natural erosion along coasts is slow. Sea cliffs tend to retreat at moderate rates because they are protected against direct wave attack by strips of beach sand along their bases. But the building of a jetty or other structure helps to block the natural movement of sand along a shore, and the sand may be stripped from a line of cliffs. With the cliffs exposed to the full force of the waves, a rapid increase in the rate of erosion can result. These effects, however, can usually be reduced if the design of such structures is guided by detailed studies of coastal erosion processes.

Major earthquakes, devastating in inland areas, are even more destructive along coasts. Buildings that would stand well on bedrock may be shaken to the ground if they are built upon artificial fill or mud flats. Special design is therefore needed for building on such unstable lands.

Seismic sea waves sweep across the ocean from earthquake areas to expend their destructive energies on distant shores. These can now be forecast in time for public warning. But local waves created by underwater landslides are a more terrible kind of event spawned by earthquakes. When submarine slides are set in motion by seismic vibrations, the water above them may be thrown into sudden violent waves. These waves can sweep onto the shore to heights of hundreds of feet above sea level. Of the 129 people who died in the 1964 Alaskan earthquake, most were killed by waves of this type. Surveys showing the location of faults near the coast and of nearby unstable sea floors may show, in advance, areas where such waves are likely to develop. These surveys can help to save many lives.

Only within the last twenty years has any great amount of information been collected from beneath the floor of the sea. Vast submarine areas still remain unexplored, yet basic ideas about the relation between the ocean basins and the earth as a whole are rapidly evolving.

Many geologists now believe that the continents have been slowly displaced with respect to the ocean basins and to each other. If this is true, proof showing the now unknown cause of this continental drift should soon be found on the sea floor.

Recalling Facts

1. What interrupts the natural movement of sand along a shore?
   - ☐ a. a jetty
   - ☐ b. low tide
   - ☐ c. a cliff

2. Compared with earthquakes inland, earthquakes along the beach are
   - ☐ a. more severe.
   - ☐ b. less severe.
   - ☐ c. the same.

3. Which one of the following is more dangerous?
   - ☐ a. seismic waves
   - ☐ b. squall waves
   - ☐ c. landslide waves

4. The Alaskan earthquake occurred during the middle
   - ☐ a. 1940s.
   - ☐ b. 1950s.
   - ☐ c. 1960s.

5. Intensive study of the ocean floor has occurred during the last
   - ☐ a. 5 years.
   - ☐ b. 10 years.
   - ☐ c. 20 years.

Understanding the Passage

6. Most of the people who died in the Alaskan earthquake were
   - ☐ a. crushed by falling buildings.
   - ☐ b. lost in the open faults of the earth.
   - ☐ c. drowned by the sea.

7. One of the author's supporting details deals with
   - ☐ a. wind erosion.
   - ☐ b. water erosion.
   - ☐ c. current erosion.

8. The author suggests that buildings along the water should
   - ☐ a. be built to withstand high winds.
   - ☐ b. not be exposed to the south or east.
   - ☐ c. be built differently from inland buildings.

9. Geologists expect to find the reason for continental movements
   - ☐ a. in the rock structures along fault lines.
   - ☐ b. in the regions of volcanic activity.
   - ☐ c. on the floor of the ocean.

10. We may conclude that
    - ☐ a. vast areas of the ocean floor have never been seen by man.
    - ☐ b. scientists have not concentrated their work in Alaska.
    - ☐ c. the forecasting of seismic sea waves is very difficult.

Going to the Woods for Water

By standing at the top of the Newark, New Jersey, watershed one can see the New York City skyline 30 miles away. Just downslope are 30,000 acres of municipal forest, a true wilderness set in the midst of the most densely populated portion of the country, the 500-mile stretch of people, traffic, noise, and rooftops that runs from Washington to Boston. The Newark forest is a water forest. Water is its principal product.

In the Northeast there are about 400 municipal watersheds with more than a million acres of forest land. The water from these watersheds serves about a third of the region's population of some fifty million.

In the West, the national forests furnish most of the water that supplies the cities and towns. Slightly more than forty million acres of national forest land are used as municipal watersheds. More than seventeen million people in almost 1,100 communities depend directly on these watersheds for all or a major part of their daily water supply. The largest municipally owned watershed in the West is the 66,000-acre portion of Seattle's Cedar River watershed.

The systems that connect forest watersheds to the cities' faucets furnish high-quality water. This is the reason for their existence. Sparsely populated forests and related wildland are stable environments. They are natural filters set into the water cycle between rainflow and streamflow. To a great degree, metropolitan areas have gone to the woods for their water. Very likely, water that reaches Eastern faucets dripped from some forest tree on its way. In the West, chances are good that it came from a melting snowbank high in the forested Rockies, Cascades, or Sierras.

Each municipal watershed has its own management problems. Baltimore, Maryland, for instance, has been purchasing land for the past fifty years around its three reservoirs and now owns about 17,000 acres.

To cut or not to cut the trees on a municipal watershed is a question that has bothered many city officials, though by now the great majority of municipalities permit cutting. At one time, commercial cutting was not permitted on any of the municipally owned land within New York City's watershed. As a result, pine plantations became very dense and showed evidence of stagnation and insect injury. Also, a no-cutting policy can sometimes reduce the yield of water. Careful management of the forests in a watershed area will assist in creating a high-yield water crop.

Recalling Facts

1. Approximately how many municipal watersheds exist in the Northeast?
   - ☐ a. 200
   - ☐ b. 400
   - ☐ c. 600

2. The 500-mile stretch of land between Washington and Boston is an area of
   - ☐ a. dense population.
   - ☐ b. heavy precipitation.
   - ☐ c. slow economic growth.

3. The Newark forest is described as a
   - ☐ a. hardwood forest.
   - ☐ b. water forest.
   - ☐ c. pine forest.

4. A city that has been buying land for fifty years is
   - ☐ a. Dallas.
   - ☐ b. Denver.
   - ☐ c. Baltimore.

5. The distance between New York City and the Newark watershed is
   - ☐ a. 10 miles.
   - ☐ b. 30 miles.
   - ☐ c. 50 miles.

Understanding the Passage

6. According to the author, very dense forests can
   - ☐ a. reduce water yield.
   - ☐ b. increase water production.
   - ☐ c. protect water from contamination.

7. Forests are important to watersheds because trees
   - ☐ a. produce moisture as they give off carbon dioxide.
   - ☐ b. absorb water vapor from the environment.
   - ☐ c. reduce evaporation of groundwater supplies.

8. Sparsely wooded forests
   - ☐ a. produce low-quality water.
   - ☐ b. filter water on its way to rivers and streams.
   - ☐ c. are usually not highly valued.

9. National forests provide the greatest amount of water for cities and towns in the
   - ☐ a. South.
   - ☐ b. Northeast.
   - ☐ c. West.

10. We can conclude that
    - ☐ a. most communities realize the value of their forest areas.
    - ☐ b. commercial tree cutting lowers the value of a forest.
    - ☐ c. many reservoirs are being constructed in forest areas.

A fire hazard is present during flooding. Electric power should be shut off. Gas jets or valves should be closed. And open flames should be doused. If power is needed, locate power lines above flood levels.

Power to electric appliances should be turned off before they are flooded. After flooding, the appliances should be cleaned and dried before being used again. Rugs and furniture should be cleaned after flooding.

Erosion of lawns and of fields can be decreased by proper placement of trees and shrubbery.

Fences and hedges can be arranged to reduce the effects of rushing floodwaters. Your county engineer, agricultural agent, or city engineer can advise you. Natural dunes along coastal areas should be kept because they provide fine protection against tidal action.

Roadbeds can be given greater protection by reducing the scouring action of floodwaters. Culverts and other openings should be large enough to handle most floods without overflowing and washing away the highway fill. Trees or shrubs can be planted on the slopes of road fills to resist washing.

If you live in a flood plain or if you have equipment in the areas subject to flooding, you should have a plan to remove valuables in times of emergency. Some goods and equipment can be lifted to higher levels in the same structure. You should be prepared to build platforms or to strengthen supports of available shelves.

You should know which roads flood at various flood heights to assure your safe escape from areas that are expected to be flooded to great depths.

Grain should be stored at levels above the floods or in structures that are flood proofed. Storage of large amounts should be at elevations above flooding.

Where the depths of flooding are not expected to be great, homes and other structures can be raised. They can be jacked up and their foundation walls raised at reasonable cost. Sometimes buildings can be moved to sites that are above the expected flood heights.

If you are building a new home, locate it free from flooding or design it to withstand any flooding with minimum losses.

In rural areas, there should be openings in the structures and in the surrounding fences or walls that will permit access to higher land for the livestock and for removing equipment.

The best time, and most economical way, to flood proof is when you build your home or other structures.

Recalling Facts

1. This article states that during floods there is a danger of
   - ☐ a. disease.
   - ☐ b. fire.
   - ☐ c. looting.

2. After a flood, electrical appliances should be
   - ☐ a. cleaned.
   - ☐ b. repaired.
   - ☐ c. thrown away.

3. Trees and shrubs help to
   - ☐ a. prevent flooding.
   - ☐ b. protect buildings.
   - ☐ c. decrease erosion.

4. County engineers
   - ☐ a. predict floods.
   - ☐ b. give advice.
   - ☐ c. build bridges.

5. The scouring action of floodwaters can be prevented
   - ☐ a. on roadbeds.
   - ☐ b. near hedges.
   - ☐ c. around livestock.

Understanding the Passage

6. When the author suggests raising a building, he or she means that
   - ☐ a. a second story should be added.
   - ☐ b. the foundation should be made higher.
   - ☐ c. it should be built on high pilings.

7. The author of this selection
   - ☐ a. gives advice on flood safety.
   - ☐ b. describes how to flood proof a new house.
   - ☐ c. suggests different ways of leaving a flooded area.

8. When flooding begins,
   - ☐ a. shrubs should be transplanted.
   - ☐ b. windows should be boarded.
   - ☐ c. power should be turned off.

9. This article does not discuss the
   - ☐ a. causes of floods.
   - ☐ b. storage of grain in flood areas.
   - ☐ c. removal of valuables during floods.

10. We can conclude that
    - ☐ a. people are now able to stop floods.
    - ☐ b. flooding occurs along ocean property.
    - ☐ c. steps can rarely be taken to reduce flood damage.

At first blush, home wine making seems about as sensible as growing wheat in a garden so one can grind flour in order to bake bread to save 90 cents.

But it doesn't matter to the rapidly growing group of home wine makers whose basements smell of every organic substance from dried rose hips to dandelions.

Home wine making antedates commercial wineries by aeons. The earliest writings describe many wines, including the Biblical mead, which is wine made from honey. But in affluent America, both home wine making and wine drinking have suffered various stigmas. Wine drinking was considered social snobbery, and wine making at home was something for the ethnics or for granny with her jug of elderberry wine.

But the winds of change are blowing even through the beer and pizza set. Commercial wineries can't plant enough grapes to keep up with wine-thirsty Americans.

Surprisingly, one of the greatest centers of interest in basement wine making is in the Upper Midwest. The largest maker of home wine-making supplies reports that not only is interest high in the North Central area, but that their largest volume store is in a Minneapolis suburb. In the Twin Cities it's almost impossible to find a bar without a waiting list for its used wine bottles.

This fascination with home wine making is probably a combination of two trends: the boom in handicrafts of all kinds and the sharp rise in the price of good wines due to increasing demand.

Home wine-making techniques today are far different from the way Aunt Clarissa made her lingonberry wine in the old cracked crock with baker's yeast left over from bread baking. The eager oenologist is armed with a miniature version of the laboratory used by commercial vintners: hydrometers, thermometers, acid titration kits, and many chemicals. His yeast is likely to be a carefully cultured wine yeast from France or Germany.

The real breakthrough in home wine making came with the availability of good fruit and grape concentrates. Up until the 1950s, most wine makers used either fresh fruit or grapes shipped from California. They took so long in transit they were nearly spoiled on arrival. They were also quite expensive.

Grape concentrates have long been used by commercial wineries for blending, especially in poor grape years. Since 1968, would-be American wine makers have been able to pluck readily from wine store shelves a host of grape and other fruit concentrates.

Recalling Facts

1. Mead is wine made from
   - ☐ a. rose hips.
   - ☐ b. barley.
   - ☐ c. honey.

2. Wine making in America was once looked upon as the work of
   - ☐ a. elderly ladies.
   - ☐ b. prison inmates.
   - ☐ c. moonshiners.

3. The art of wine making is called
   - ☐ a. graphology.
   - ☐ b. oenology.
   - ☐ c. paleontology.

4. One of the greatest centers of interest in wine making is the
   - ☐ a. Upper Midwest.
   - ☐ b. Deep South.
   - ☐ c. New England states.

5. Carefully cultured wine yeast comes from
   - ☐ a. Denmark.
   - ☐ b. Italy.
   - ☐ c. Germany.

Understanding the Passage

6. Until recently, the greatest drawback to home wine making has been
   - ☐ a. the difficulty in acquiring quality grapes.
   - ☐ b. state laws against home stills.
   - ☐ c. a shortage of yeast.

7. At first thought, home wine making
   - ☐ a. seems like a very good idea.
   - ☐ b. makes little sense.
   - ☐ c. sounds like an inexpensive hobby.

8. Commercial wineries have difficulty
   - ☐ a. keeping up with demands for wine.
   - ☐ b. growing quality grapes.
   - ☐ c. finding enough bottles for their product.

9. The sudden fascination with home wine making can be attributed to the
   - ☐ a. extensive advertising of wine making kits.
   - ☐ b. interest in making things by hand.
   - ☐ c. low cost of wine making supplies.

10. We can conclude that
   - ☐ a. wine must have a certain temperature sometime in the brewing process.
   - ☐ b. making wine at home requires much time and patience.
   - ☐ c. dandelions make the sweetest wine.

31 The Mystery of Migration

The migration of birds usually refers to the regular flights between their summer and winter homes. Except for those that nest in the tropics, nearly all North American birds migrate. Some travel great distances while others go only a short way.

This seasonal movement has long been a mystery to man. Aristotle, the naturalist and philosopher of ancient Greece, noticed that cranes, pelicans, geese, swans, doves, and many other birds moved to warmer places to spend the winter. His ideas began superstitions that lasted for hundreds of years. For example, Aristotle thought that many birds spent the winter sleeping in hollow trees, caves, or beneath the mud in marshes.

Many scientists believe that birds migrate north to south because of inclement weather. These birds began this journey originally because they were driven southward by the advancing ice age.

Another theory holds that birds migrate to areas where insects are plentiful. Many birds feed almost entirely upon insects. When winter arrives, insects disappear and the birds would starve unless they moved southward. It is puzzling, then, that insect eaters fly north again with the coming of spring.

A more realistic theory is that birds have a lasting impression of their birthplace, resulting in a lifelong urge to return to this locale each spring.

Recently scientists have found that length of day is the triggering force that prepares many birds for their migratory journeys. The change in length of day brings the birds into breeding condition and causes them to seek their northern nesting grounds.

In North America, it is possible to see migrating birds almost every month of the year. Some birds start south early in July, while others remain north until pushed out by either severe weather or shortage of food. Soon after hardy travelers reach winter homes, other equally hardy migrants start north on the heels of winter. Some early spring migrants arrive too soon, are caught in sudden storms, and may perish.

Many birds migrate by night. Although most birds seem helpless in the dark, there are good reasons for this nighttime travel. Some are poor fliers. Even good fliers can fall easy prey to hawks, who feed and migrate in daylight. Also, night migrants have daylight hours for feeding.

Many kinds of wading and swimming birds migrate either by day or night. Such birds usually feed at all hours and rarely depend on hiding to escape enemies.

Recalling Facts

1. Most North American birds migrate except for those in
   - ☐ a. the northeast.
   - ☐ b. the tropics.
   - ☐ c. swampy areas.

2. The author mentions the observations of
   - ☐ a. Socrates.
   - ☐ b. Aristophanes.
   - ☐ c. Aristotle.

3. Originally, birds began their migrations because of
   - ☐ a. food shortages.
   - ☐ b. advancing ice.
   - ☐ c. genetic weaknesses.

4. The triggering force that prepares birds for migration is
   - ☐ a. length of day.
   - ☐ b. stormy weather.
   - ☐ c. change of temperature.

5. Some birds begin to move south as early as
   - ☐ a. July.
   - ☐ b. August.
   - ☐ c. September.

Understanding the Passage

6. The author suggests that many people associate migration with
   - ☐ a. changes in climate.
   - ☐ b. animal migrations.
   - ☐ c. superstitions.

7. Generally, birds migrate at night because they
   - ☐ a. see better in the dark.
   - ☐ b. find more food at night.
   - ☐ c. are safer in the dark.

8. The author implies that wading and swimming birds are
   - ☐ a. less timid.
   - ☐ b. very timid.
   - ☐ c. very brave.

9. Birds return to northern homes in spring because
   - ☐ a. food is more plentiful.
   - ☐ b. instinct drives them to their birthplace.
   - ☐ c. southern areas become crowded with many species.

10. We can conclude that
    - ☐ a. birds are able to sense changes in weather.
    - ☐ b. all migrating birds are skillful fliers.
    - ☐ c. bird migration is not completely understood.

Life insurance is financial protection for dependents against financial loss as a result of the breadwinner's death. Because today's families depend on cash, life insurance is a way through which families can gain protection and financial security.

Life insurance is neither a savings plan nor an investment plan. It is meant to be mainly an educational fund for children.

When the breadwinner dies, there are many financial problems a family must face. The problems usually include burial expenses and any medical expenses not covered by health insurance, adequate funds to meet the family's living expenses until the spouse or children can make employment arrangements, and educational funds for children.

Regardless of the frills and fanfare about life insurance policies, there are four basic types of life insurance: term, straight life, limited payment life, and endowment.

Term insurance provides pure protection while the other three have a savings feature. The basic principle is to gain the most protection for the family at the lowest cost.

Term insurance is a type of life insurance that provides pure protection only. As the name implies, the policy covers the owner of the policy for a term of 1, 5, 10, or 20 years. At the end of the term, the coverage stops, and the policy has no cash value.

Term insurance is the type of insurance that gives the family the greatest amount of protection for a limited period for the least cost. It generally is best to buy term insurance on a reducing coverage basis so that it can be reduced or terminated as dependents become older and no longer require as much protection.

Term insurance can be increased to the maximum protection as each child is born or can be decreased to no insurance on the parent as the children become economically independent. Several term policies rather than one or two large policies can be bought. This allows the policyholder to increase coverage or to drop policies to best meet his or her needs.

Straight life insurance provides for a certain amount of coverage throughout life. It differs from term insurance in that straight life combines a decreasing amount of protection with an increasing amount of savings in the policy. Because of the savings element as well as the protection in the straight life plan, the premium for a certain amount of straight life at a given age is higher than the premium for term insurance.

Recalling Facts

1. One life insurance policy is called
   - ☐ a. investment insurance.
   - ☐ b. savings plan life insurance.
   - ☐ c. endowment insurance.

2. Term insurance covers the owner for a maximum term of
   - ☐ a. ten years.
   - ☐ b. twenty years.
   - ☐ c. thirty years.

3. The least expensive type of insurance is
   - ☐ a. straight life.
   - ☐ b. term.
   - ☐ c. limited payment life.

4. Protection under a straight life policy
   - ☐ a. increases as a person ages.
   - ☐ b. decreases as a person ages.
   - ☐ c. remains constant as a person ages.

5. How many basic types of life insurance are offered?
   - ☐ a. three
   - ☐ b. four
   - ☐ c. five

Understanding the Passage

6. The author is critical of
   - ☐ a. glorified advertising for life insurance policies.
   - ☐ b. people who buy several small policies instead of one large one.
   - ☐ c. companies that charge customers twice for the same premium.

7. The reader can infer that
   - ☐ a. term insurance can be purchased by the head of the household only.
   - ☐ b. limited payment life insurance is like a savings account.
   - ☐ c. straight life insurance is a good investment for the retirement years.

8. After a term policy is bought, it
   - ☐ a. can be dropped by the owner at any time.
   - ☐ b. cannot be canceled by the owner.
   - ☐ c. can be revoked by the company.

9. The content of this selection can best be described as
   - ☐ a. entertaining.
   - ☐ b. informative.
   - ☐ c. misleading.

10. According to the author,
    - ☐ a. most life insurance policies provide protection and some financial security.
    - ☐ b. many life insurance policies provide protection only.
    - ☐ c. some life insurance policies provide financial security only.

Residents of the Ozarks foothills have swapped damaging floodwaters for a large fishing lake, a state park, and an excellent waterfowl refuge. And they have beautified the lakeshore with dogwood and redbud plantings.

Who is benefiting from this exchange? Tourists certainly are. But the folks from the Flat Creek watershed in northeastern Arkansas are reaping more benefits, too.

In any case, this is a good example of how the recreation developments in small watershed projects are helping to meet the ever-rising demand for more public water-related recreation in our nation.

Today, in the Flat Creek watershed, the tourists and residents alike enjoy boating, swimming, fishing, camping, picnicking, and a variety of other activities. Besides all this water-based fun, there are some solid economic returns. What's more, migratory ducks and geese by the thousands have a first-class stopping place.

But one must go back to the beginning of a success story that really holds water!

The problem in the Flat Creek region of Lawrence County in the low, rolling foothills of the Ozark Mountains was "too much or too little."

Farmers had too much water. Flooding usually occurred about four times each year, damaging the crops, buildings, and roads. Flooding interrupted travel for schoolbuses and mail and milk routes. Gullied lands in the upland section of the watershed contributed to the flood problem by filling the drainageways with sediment. Average annual losses amounted to about $60,000.

Yet nearby was the Arkansas Game and Fish Commission's 1,000-acre Shirey Bay-Rainey Brake Wildlife Refuge that often needed extra water. This water was needed to accommodate the more than 15,000 ducks and geese that stop there daily during their migrations. These bottom and hardwood lands are ideal resting and feeding grounds for migratory waterfowl. But during years of low rainfall in late summer and early fall, the area is extremely dry. This dryness is a frequent problem.

A solution to this problem was to get the water off the farmers' fields and store it until needed for the wildlife refuge. Through the Lawrence County Soil Conservation District, the landowners and the Arkansas Game and Fish Commission teamed up as cosponsors of the Flat Creek watershed project under the Watershed Protection and Flood Prevention Act. This project is known as the Small Watershed Act.

By developing this watershed, dangerous and costly flood damages are replaced by unlimited recreational opportunities and economic returns.

Recalling Facts

1. The Flat Creek watershed is
   located in
   ☐ a. Arkansas.
   ☐ b. Colorado.
   ☐ c. Iowa.

2. In the Ozark Mountains
   flooding usually occurred
   ☐ a. twice a year.
   ☐ b. three times a year.
   ☐ c. four times a year.

3. Before the watershed was
   built, flood losses in Flat
   Creek amounted to more than
   ☐ a. $50,000.
   ☐ b. $100,000.
   ☐ c. $200,000.

4. Rainfall in the Flat Creek area
   is lightest during
   ☐ a. spring.
   ☐ b. summer.
   ☐ c. winter.

5. The Flat Creek watershed
   project has provided
   ☐ a. irrigation for dry fields.
   ☐ b. a hydroelectric
       power plant.
   ☐ c. recreational facilities.

Understanding the Passage

6. This article could have
   been titled
   ☐ a. When It Rains, It Pours.
   ☐ b. Battle of the Budget.
   ☐ c. Migratory Waterfowl.

7. According to the article, the
   residents of Flat Creek built
   ☐ a. a waterfowl refuge.
   ☐ b. devices to control the flow
       of rainwater.
   ☐ c. a flood observation office.

8. The outdoor sports activities in
   the Flat Creek watershed
   ☐ a. create a traffic problem
       during summer months.
   ☐ b. draw people from all over
       the country.
   ☐ c. provide extra income for
       the area.

9. Farmers approved of the
   watershed because they could
   ☐ a. keep their fields dry.
   ☐ b. divert badly needed water to
       their crops.
   ☐ c. open their ponds to
       recreational fishing.

10. The Flat Creek watershed has
    attracted many birds because
    ☐ a. the area contains many
        varieties of grains and seeds.
    ☐ b. they migrate through
        the area.
    ☐ c. the land is very wet during
        the rainy season.

34 The Stormy Season

The direct rays of the sun touch the equator and strike northward toward the Tropic of Cancer. In the southern hemisphere winter has begun, and it is summer north of the equator. The sea and air grow warmer; the polar air of winter begins its gradual retreat.

The northward shift of the sun also brings the season of tropical cyclones to the northern hemisphere, a season that is ending for the Pacific and Indian Oceans south of the equator. Along our coasts and those of Asia, it is time to look seaward, to guard against the season's storms. Over the Pacific, the tropical cyclone season is never quite over, but varies in intensity. Every year, conditions east of the Philippines send a score of violent storms howling toward Asia, but it is worst from June through October. Southwest of Mexico, a few Pacific hurricanes will grow during spring and summer, but most will die at sea or perish over the desert or strike the lower California coast as squalls.

Along our Atlantic and Gulf coasts, the hurricane season is from June to November. In an average year, there are fewer than ten tropical cyclones and six of them will develop into hurricanes. These will kill 50 to 100 persons between Texas and Maine and cause property damage of more than $100 million. If the year is worse than average, we will suffer several hundred deaths, and property damage will run to billions of dollars.

Tornadoes, floods, and severe storms are in season elsewhere on the continent. Now, to these destructive forces must be added the hazard of the hurricane.

From the National Hurricane Center in Miami, a radar fence reaches westward to Texas and northward to New England. It provides a 200-mile look into offshore disturbances. In Maryland, the giant computers of the National Meteorological Center digest the myriad bits of data—atmospheric pressure, temperature, humidity, surface winds, and winds aloft—received from weather stations and ships monitoring the atmospheric setting each hour, every day. Cloud photographs from spacecraft orbiting the earth are received in Maryland and are studied for the telltale spiral on the warming sea. The crews of United States aircraft over the Gulf of Mexico, Caribbean, and Atlantic watch the sky and wait for the storm that will bear a person's name. The machinery of early warning vibrates with new urgency as the season of great storms begins.

Recalling Facts

1. How many hurricanes occur annually along the Atlantic and Gulf coasts?
   - ☐ a. two
   - ☐ b. four
   - ☐ c. six

2. Property damage during an average hurricane season amounts to
   - ☐ a. $100 million.
   - ☐ b. $150 million.
   - ☐ c. $200 million.

3. The National Hurricane Center is located in
   - ☐ a. Washington, D.C.
   - ☐ b. Atlanta.
   - ☐ c. Miami.

4. Radar at the National Hurricane Center can track storms
   - ☐ a. 200 miles away.
   - ☐ b. 400 miles away.
   - ☐ c. 600 miles away.

5. The hurricane season in the Atlantic lasts from June to
   - ☐ a. September.
   - ☐ b. October.
   - ☐ c. November.

Understanding the Passage

6. The author implies that hurricanes southwest of Mexico
   - ☐ a. are not very dangerous.
   - ☐ b. take many lives each year.
   - ☐ c. move toward Japan.

7. The facts in the article suggest that
   - ☐ a. cyclones are more numerous north of the equator.
   - ☐ b. the Philippines are hit by many storms.
   - ☐ c. hurricanes can develop over warm waters only.

8. The author points out that
   - ☐ a. cyclones usually move in a northerly direction.
   - ☐ b. Pacific cyclones develop throughout the year.
   - ☐ c. hurricanes kill more people than any other storms.

9. In one paragraph, the author implies that
   - ☐ a. hurricanes are more severe than cyclones.
   - ☐ b. cyclones have the same intensity as hurricanes.
   - ☐ c. hurricanes have never struck Europe.

10. We can conclude that
    - ☐ a. complex equipment is used in hurricane forecasts.
    - ☐ b. hurricanes often strike land without warning.
    - ☐ c. Florida is hit by more hurricanes than any other state.

Profit by Prophecy

The occult business flourishes because people are naturally curious about the unusual. Today's occult prophets, channelers, and practitioners are far more fortunate than their historical counterparts. Throughout the ages, it was punishable by torture or death to predict the death or succession of royalty.

The poor soothsayer, however removed from personal gain, was held responsible in some way for his messages. For instance, Emperor Tiberius had a habit of walking with his astrologer and a servant along the cliffs, asking for signs and meanings. If the stars happened to be against Tiberius, the astrologer was thrown over the cliff.

Ancient Romans weren't the only unlucky star readers. In the 14th century, a German was burned at the stake for poisoning wells after warning of their danger, a logical connection of sorts. But truth of the hapless man's prediction turned out to be the Black Plague.

Englishman William Lily, in 1666, predicted a fire and was arrested for arson when it occurred. Fortunately Lily was released after the Great Fire of London finally burned itself out.

Witches have been punished throughout history. Often, however, witchcraft was little more than nature worship. That a Satanic interest developed isn't surprising, considering the linkage of nature, pastoral settings, and fertility festivals.

The witches who were hunted between 1450 and 1750 were not simple peasants, as far as God's earthly servants were concerned. Witches belonged to a subversive force working to undermine the Church. Siding with Satan was an unthinkable crime, and witchcraft symbolized the overthrow of God.

One would not want to read Tarot cards in a time when flaying, frying, and repeatedly raising someone into the air and dropping him to the ground were the more humane methods to gain confessions of witchcraft involvement.

A woman in Scotland was burned as a witch because she was seen stroking a cat in an open window at the same time a housekeeper's brew turned stale. A Boston immigrant of Irish nationality who prayed in Latin was hanged as a witch because she could not repeat the prayers in English. Many women were punished for crimes they did not commit.

Twentieth-century occult fans can be happy the business climate is not as harsh as in olden times, but even today, profit by prophecy is considered by some to be unholy. The standing rule seems to be "If you have power, and profit selfishly, it is ill-gotten profit."

*Reading Time*_____ *Comprehension Score*_____ *Words per Minute*_____

Recalling Facts

1. The occult business flourishes because people are basically
   - ☐ a. skeptical.
   - ☐ b. religious.
   - ☐ c. curious.

2. In ancient times, soothsayers seldom predicted
   - ☐ a. misfortunes.
   - ☐ b. financial matters.
   - ☐ c. marriages.

3. Emperor Tiberius walked with his astrologers
   - ☐ a. in the forest.
   - ☐ b. around the moat.
   - ☐ c. along the cliffs.

4. In the 14th century, a German was burned at the stake for
   - ☐ a. poisoning wells.
   - ☐ b. reading tea leaves.
   - ☐ c. stealing maps.

5. The woman who was accused of causing brew to turn stale lived in
   - ☐ a. Scotland.
   - ☐ b. England.
   - ☐ c. France.

Understanding the Passage

6. The author mentions the Great Fire of London as an example of
   - ☐ a. a disaster caused by human carelessness.
   - ☐ b. an exaggeration of an actual event.
   - ☐ c. a catastrophe that was accurately predicted.

7. The Black Plague was
   - ☐ a. forecast accurately by a famous writer.
   - ☐ b. spread by contaminated water.
   - ☐ c. thought to be the work of the Devil.

8. An occult prophet in today's world does not worry about being
   - ☐ a. ridiculed for a prediction that does not come true.
   - ☐ b. accused of undermining the doctrine of the church.
   - ☐ c. tortured for a false prediction.

9. The author implies that
   - ☐ a. people who predict the future are usually ill.
   - ☐ b. most astrologers use Tarot cards.
   - ☐ c. some prophecies come true.

10. The reader can conclude that
    - ☐ a. innocent people have been killed as witches.
    - ☐ b. most witches are convinced that they can cast spells.
    - ☐ c. Tarot cards can predict the future with accuracy.

When English settlers founded Jamestown Colony in 1607, Virginia was occupied by a group of Algonquin Indian tribes headed by a powerful chief known as Powhatan. Although Chief Powhatan could easily have destroyed the entire young colony, he and his people were friendly during the pioneers' first difficult years.

Captain John Smith, the English colony's leader, described Powhatan as a tall, dignified man with a grim, suspicious face and a reputation for cruelty to anyone who got in his way.

But Powhatan had a very soft heart for his dearest daughter, Pocahontas, a girl of about 13 at the time of the English arrival.

Many legends center around Pocahontas. One of the most famous tells that when John Smith, having gone too far into Indian territory, was captured and about to be beheaded at Powhatan's order, Pocahontas saved his life by throwing herself over his body. Then Powhatan, yielding to Pocahontas's pleas, pardoned the English leader and sent him back to Jamestown in peace.

In 1609, making a diplomatic effort to keep the Indians' goodwill, the English settlers crowned Chief Powhatan king of the territory. Much pomp and ceremony went along with the crowning, but it was not a complete success. Powhatan was more interested in the gifts that went along with the event than in the crown itself. He was reluctant to bow his head even long enough for the crown to be placed upon it.

The relations between the Indians and the settlers became less friendly after John Smith's return to England, and promises were broken on both sides. The English intruded upon Indian lands, and the resentful Powhatan captured settlers and stole colonists' belongings. There were several years of minor warfare.

In 1613, taking advantage of Powhatan's great love for his daughter, the English lured Pocahontas onto a British ship and carried her off to Jamestown. With so valuable a hostage, the settlers were able to arrange ransom terms. English prisoners and goods were returned, and Pocahontas was restored to her father.

But while she was living among the English at Jamestown, Pocahontas had met John Rolfe, an honest and good man. They fell in love. After Pocahontas had been converted to Christianity and baptized under the name of "the Lady Rebecca," she and Rolfe were married.

The match was much to the benefit of English colonists, for Powhatan kept peace with them until his death in 1618.

Recalling Facts

1. When the Jamestown Colony was being founded, the Algonquins were
   - ☐ a. friendly.
   - ☐ b. helpful.
   - ☐ c. hostile.

2. Powhatan was described by Captain John Smith as
   - ☐ a. grim.
   - ☐ b. sly.
   - ☐ c. uncivilized.

3. When the English arrived to settle Jamestown, Pocahontas was
   - ☐ a. thirteen.
   - ☐ b. eighteen.
   - ☐ c. twenty-one.

4. Powhatan died
   - ☐ a. before 1620.
   - ☐ b. in 1625.
   - ☐ c. after 1630.

5. Pocahontas became known as the
   - ☐ a. Lady Helena.
   - ☐ b. Lady Rebecca.
   - ☐ c. Lady Virginia.

Understanding the Passage

6. The author does not explain
   - ☐ a. how Powhatan died.
   - ☐ b. whom Pocahontas married.
   - ☐ c. where Pocahontas was taken as a hostage.

7. The marriage of Pocahontas
   - ☐ a. caused much grief in England.
   - ☐ b. worsened English-Indian relations.
   - ☐ c. ensured peace between colonists and Indians.

8. The author presents the legend about Pocahontas and Captain John Smith
   - ☐ a. with much skepticism.
   - ☐ b. with proof to support the story.
   - ☐ c. without any elaboration.

9. The author portrays Powhatan as a
   - ☐ a. materialistic person.
   - ☐ b. rude host.
   - ☐ c. loving husband.

10. This article is mostly concerned with
    - ☐ a. legends of the first colonial settlements.
    - ☐ b. relations between early colonists and the Indians.
    - ☐ c. British rule in the American colonies.

Crossroads of the World

The Isthmus of Panama, colonized by the Spanish in the early 1500s, became the crossroads of Spanish America with the conquest in 1533 of the Incan empire by Francisco Pizzaro. Gold, silver, and other treasures from Peru and elsewhere on the Pacific coast of Central and South America were taken each year to what is now the "old city" of Panama on the Pacific side of the Isthmus. Then they were transported by horse and mule over the Royal Road to Portobelo on the Atlantic coast where they were loaded aboard galleons of Spain's treasure fleet. Storms and pirates took a heavy toll of ships and treasure between Panama and Spain. ●

Nearly four centuries later, Panama became the crossroads of the world with the opening of the Panama Canal in 1914. The fifty-mile-long waterway across the Isthmus eliminated the need for thousands of miles of travel around Cape Horn for sea traffic between the Atlantic and Pacific Oceans.

The Canal Zone bisects not only the Isthmus but the Republic of Panama as well. The Zone, which is about 65 miles long and ten miles wide, is administered by the Canal Zone government under a governor appointed by the President of the United States. About 42,000 persons live ● in the Zone, mostly employees of the Zone government and Canal company, members of the armed forces, and their families.

Because of the curved shape of the Isthmus, the Pacific entrance of the Canal is 27 miles east, not west, of the Atlantic entrance.

Ships of all nations use the Canal, and transits through the waterway number over 12,000 annually. The Canal's strategic importance to the United States is underlined by the fact that our navy's fleet units, as well as ships carrying defense cargoes, can be quickly shifted between the Atlantic and Pacific Oceans. For example, the canal reduces the voyage ● from New York to San Francisco by 7,873 miles. This voyage saves three weeks' sailing time by a fifteen-knot ship.

The U.S. government began construction of the Canal in 1904, after buying the rights and property of a French company that had made a valiant but unsuccessful attempt to do the job. Construction took ten years, and the successful campaign against malaria and yellow fever conducted in the swamp of the Isthmus was as important to the success of the canal-building venture as the complex engineering feats performed.

Recalling Facts

1. The Isthmus of Panama was colonized by the
   - ☐ a. Dutch.
   - ☐ b. Portuguese.
   - ☐ c. Spanish.

2. The Incas were conquered during the
   - ☐ a. 1400s.
   - ☐ b. 1500s.
   - ☐ c. 1600s.

3. The Panama Canal was opened to navigation in
   - ☐ a. 1845.
   - ☐ b. 1914.
   - ☐ c. 1932.

4. According to the author, the length of the Canal is
   - ☐ a. 12 miles.
   - ☐ b. 36 miles.
   - ☐ c. 50 miles.

5. The United States purchased the Canal property from
   - ☐ a. Spain.
   - ☐ b. France.
   - ☐ c. Mexico.

Understanding the Passage

6. A ship moving through the Canal toward the Pacific Ocean would travel
   - ☐ a. north.
   - ☐ b. east.
   - ☐ c. west.

7. The greatest obstacle to the completion of the Canal was the
   - ☐ a. difficulty in moving supplies to the digging site.
   - ☐ b. inability to find workers to continue the project.
   - ☐ c. continual outbreak of disease.

8. The author implies that the Canal is important to the U.S. for
   - ☐ a. inexpensive tourist cruises.
   - ☐ b. trade with foreign countries.
   - ☐ c. easy mobilization of war ships.

9. A ship that travels through the Canal instead of sailing around Cape Horn
   - ☐ a. saves several weeks' sailing time.
   - ☐ b. incurs greater expenses.
   - ☐ c. receives clearance from the U.S. Navy.

10. We can conclude that the Panama Canal is
    - ☐ a. used regularly by many countries.
    - ☐ b. operated by the Republic of Panama.
    - ☐ c. battered often by tropical storms.

The Great Ice Age was a period of many widespread glacier formations. During this time, mountain glaciers formed on all continents. The ice caps of Antarctica and Greenland were more extensive and thicker than today. And vast glaciers, in places as much as several thousand feet thick, spread across northern North America and Eurasia.

Almost a third of the present land surface of the Earth was ice covered. Even today remnants of the great glaciers cover almost a tenth of the land. This indicates that conditions similar to those that produced the Great Ice Age are still operating in polar climates.

Much has been learned about the Great Ice Age glaciers because evidence of their presence is widespread. Similar conditions can be studied today in Greenland, Antarctica, and in many mountain ranges where glaciers still exist. It is possible, therefore, to reconstruct in large part the extent and general nature of the glaciers of the past, as well as to interpret their impact on the physical and biological environments.

Historically, the climate has changed periodically, just as the general character of the earth's surface has changed. There is evidence that at times in the past glacier formations occurred long before the Great Ice Age.

Following a period of warm climate, a worldwide refrigeration initiated the Great Ice Age glaciers. The climate was cooler and wetter and at times warmer and drier than today. Many attempts have been made to account for these climatic changes. Their ultimate cause, however, is not well understood. Although we cannot predict a period of climatic cooling, another ice age in the future is a possibility.

Although the Great Ice Age began a million or more years ago, the last major ice sheet to spread across the north-central United States reached its maximum extent about 20,000 years ago. It lingered in Canada until about 6,000 years ago, when it finally disappeared by melting. Mountain glaciers are today the only remnants of the great glaciers of the past on the mainland of North America.

Prior to the 19th century, observant Swiss peasants concluded that the glaciers in the Alps had formerly been much larger and had extended much farther down the mountain valleys. They noted that the existing glaciers were slowly transporting and depositing boulders downvalley. They correctly inferred that the boulders strewn about their pastures had been transported and deposited in the same manner long ago.

Recalling Facts

1. What fraction of the surface was once covered by ice?
   - ☐ a. one-third
   - ☐ b. one-half
   - ☐ c. three-quarters

2. Even today glaciers cover how much of the land surface?
   - ☐ a. one-quarter
   - ☐ b. one-fifth
   - ☐ c. one-tenth

3. Glaciers still can be studied today in
   - ☐ a. the United States.
   - ☐ b. Grenada.
   - ☐ c. Greenland.

4. How many years ago did the United States glacier reach its peak?
   - ☐ a. 20,000
   - ☐ b. 60,000
   - ☐ c. 100,000

5. The author feels that another ice age is
   - ☐ a. probable.
   - ☐ b. unlikely.
   - ☐ c. possible.

Understanding the Passage

6. Great Ice Age glaciers occurred after
   - ☐ a. shifts in the upper wind system were completed.
   - ☐ b. a period of warm climate ended.
   - ☐ c. polar regions became briefly tropical.

7. The author feels that the Swiss peasants were
   - ☐ a. perceptive.
   - ☐ b. easily deceived.
   - ☐ c. foolish.

8. Changes in glacier size today are most commonly noted in
   - ☐ a. central Siberia.
   - ☐ b. North Polar regions.
   - ☐ c. high mountain areas.

9. The ice sheet at Antarctica today is proof that
   - ☐ a. ice once covered the world.
   - ☐ b. ice age conditions are still operating.
   - ☐ c. heavy snows produce glaciers.

10. From this article we can conclude that
    - ☐ a. the climate of an area changes little from year to year.
    - ☐ b. the glaciers of Antarctica are continuing to melt and recede.
    - ☐ c. a cooling down of the earth could initiate another ice age.

39 Cataracts

A cataract is a cloudiness in the lens of the eye that interferes with vision. As a cataract forms, the normally clear lens becomes opaque. This partially blocks the passage of light to the retina, the tissue at the back of the eye that transmits visual impulses to the brain.

Fortunately, cataracts do not mean blindness for most people. Cataract surgery to restore vision is successful in 95 percent of cases and is possible in very elderly patients if their general health is good.

Cataract extraction can be performed with either a general or local anesthetic. Prior to surgery, medications to prevent nausea and induce drowsiness are administered. Eye drops to cleanse and numb the eyes are also used. By the time the operation begins, the patient is relaxed and comfortable. Patients usually feel no discomfort during surgery and, at most, only a dull ache afterward.

Cataracts cannot be treated with drops or other medications, and there is no way of preventing the cataracts associated with advanced age.

It is no longer considered necessary to wait until a cataract is totally opaque to perform surgery. In fact, an overly mature cataract can make extraction more difficult. Surgery may not be advised, however, for patients with other eye conditions.

The timing of the operation depends upon the patient's particular visual requirements. When both eyes are affected, doctors often try to schedule separate operations so that the patient has the use of one eye at all times. After removal of the lens, eyeglasses enable a patient to read and to perform his daily activities quite normally. Contact lenses give the best visual correction, and the possibility of wearing them should be discussed with the doctor.

If there is a cataract in only one eye and it is removed, the images seen may not fuse. Therefore, doctors sometimes recommend waiting until the cataract develops in the second eye before performing surgery.

Cataracts occur more often among people over 55 than in younger persons. Conditions other than aging, however, may also cause cataracts. Children are sometimes born with them as a result of genetic or prenatal factors. Diabetes, radiation exposure, and injuries to the lens may also cause cataracts. Although the exact reason for cataract development is not established, research is underway to identify the cause by learning more about the metabolism of the lens. The ultimate goal of such research is the prevention of this disease.

Recalling Facts

1. Cataracts form on the
   - ☐ a. retina.
   - ☐ b. pupil.
   - ☐ c. lens.

2. In what percentage of cases is cataract surgery successful?
   - ☐ a. 35 percent
   - ☐ b. 65 percent
   - ☐ c. 95 percent

3. After surgery, some patients are bothered by a
   - ☐ a. sharp pain.
   - ☐ b. dull ache.
   - ☐ c. throbbing sensation.

4. Cataracts are most often caused by
   - ☐ a. polluted air.
   - ☐ b. aging.
   - ☐ c. poor nutrition.

5. What gives the best visual correction after a cataract operation?
   - ☐ a. contact lenses
   - ☐ b. eyeglasses
   - ☐ c. bifocals

Understanding the Passage

6. Patients requesting surgery for a cataract in one eye may be told to
   - ☐ a. use eyedrops to cure the condition.
   - ☐ b. change their diets and exercise their eyes.
   - ☐ c. wait until a cataract forms in the other eye.

7. According to the article, elderly people are
   - ☐ a. usually advised against cataract operations.
   - ☐ b. fearful of eye surgery.
   - ☐ c. often operated on for cataracts.

8. The author points out that
   - ☐ a. people who are avid readers develop cataracts.
   - ☐ b. cataracts cannot be prevented.
   - ☐ c. the cause of cataracts is unknown.

9. Compared to a partial cataract, a well-developed cataract is
   - ☐ a. quite easy to remove.
   - ☐ b. more difficult to remove.
   - ☐ c. impossible to remove.

10. We can conclude that cataract operations are
    - ☐ a. safe.
    - ☐ b. expensive.
    - ☐ c. painful.

40   Refuse or Resource?

The solid waste problem has been creeping up for years, and now the glacier is upon us. Major cities are running out of landfill space. Open dumps are being closed by law. Open burning is banned. City incinerators have grown old under a very inadequate replacement and modernization program. And each day the mountain of solid waste that must be disposed of grows larger.

The United States generates over four billion tons of solid waste a year. More than 90 percent is composed of agricultural and mining wastes. About three percent is from industrial wastes and much of this mill scrap is recycled—some without leaving the plant. The toughest problem is the 250 million tons of garbage and refuse spewed from homes, schools, office buildings, stores, hospitals, towns, and villages.

This mass of metals, paper, food, grass clippings, plastic, rubber, and glass that winds up at a landfill or incinerator pit all mixed together seems of no use to anyone.

Or is it? Scattered efforts across the country indicate that new technology, properly applied, might someday turn these millions of tons of refuse into an excellent source of raw materials for new uses.

Some cities use powerful magnets to pull "tin" cans and other steel objects from solid wastes. The metal is sold to steel mills, zinc recovery operations, or copper companies.

Several new projects are studying the possibility of treating municipal wastes through pyrolysis—a system of reducing refuse to basic chemicals, liquids, and gases that have commercial value.

Another aspect of the waste removal problem is collection and transportation, which account for about 80 percent of the bill, now over six billion dollars a year.

Increasing use of heavy compactor trucks helps. Using transfer stations where a number of route collection trucks can dump into giant trailers for haulage to distant landfills also helps. In Florida, a pneumatic tube system provides automatic transport of refuse to a central collection building.

In short, many new ideas are being tested, and many will be needed, since no one method is likely to prove suitable for every community.

However, many tough economic and social questions must be answered before real progress can be made. Can recovered materials compete with new materials? What incentives will be needed to make resource recovery work? Will citizens pay the costs of changing our waste system?

Finding the answers to these questions may be the most difficult part of the task.

Recalling Facts

1. The author compares the solid waste problem to
   - ☐ a. a glacier.
   - ☐ b. a runaway train.
   - ☐ c. an insect.

2. How many billion tons of solid waste does the United States generate yearly?
   - ☐ a. two
   - ☐ b. four
   - ☐ c. six

3. Which one of the following is not cited as an example of solid waste?
   - ☐ a. grass clippings
   - ☐ b. rubber
   - ☐ c. raw sewage

4. What are some cities using to retrieve steel objects from wastes?
   - ☐ a. powerful magnets
   - ☐ b. special bulldozers
   - ☐ c. large cranes

5. In what state is a pneumatic tube system used to transport wastes?
   - ☐ a. California
   - ☐ b. Utah
   - ☐ c. Florida

Understanding the Passage

6. The article suggests that garbage and refuse from homes and public places
   - ☐ a. comprise the largest percentage of solid wastes.
   - ☐ b. are a small percentage of the total output of solid wastes.
   - ☐ c. are not really considered in the solid waste problem.

7. The process known as pyrolysis
   - ☐ a. recycles scrap from industry.
   - ☐ b. reduces refuse into its basic parts.
   - ☐ c. changes solid waste into landfill.

8. The stumbling block to progress in solid waste disposal and reuse is
   - ☐ a. economic and social.
   - ☐ b. political and industrial.
   - ☐ c. governmental and institutional.

9. To make her point, the author uses
   - ☐ a. an emotional appeal.
   - ☐ b. factual information.
   - ☐ c. propaganda techniques.

10. This article shows that
   - ☐ a. some communities are solving their waste disposal problems.
   - ☐ b. the federal government is indifferent to the problem of wastes.
   - ☐ c. open dumps are slowly solving the dilemma of solid waste disposal.

41   Construction Queries

From early childhood we are conditioned by rhyme, story, and song to the importance of strong, sturdy construction. This requirement has been drummed into our consciousness from the tragedy of the two little pigs who built their homes of sticks and straw to the storming of an impregnable castle when knights were bold and fortresses were meant to withstand everything short of nuclear weapons.

As we mature and take on the responsibilities of job and family, we are often beset with the task of building our own homes, our own castles. This is an awesome task. It is frequently the largest single investment we will ever make.

Again we think of the lesson of the three little pigs and we are bent on finding the builder who will construct our house to withstand the ravages of use and time. Today more than ever, our castle must be strong, and hence we commence our quest for the team of experts capable of transforming our plans into reality.

If an individual has already purchased and paid for a lot and has acquired the plans and specifications for a dream home, the next step is to hire a building contractor to produce it.

In the event you have engaged complete architectural services for your home, your architect is in a position to recommend builders who have undertaken similar projects and who are reliable, reputable, and good builders. If this is not the case, however, one will have to rely on recommendations from friends and others who have recently had something built.

Perhaps an individual has had a previous successful experience with a building contracting firm in the community or has friends or acquaintances who have recently completed their homes and have been pleased with the contractor's results. If this is the case, the search for a builder may be of short duration.

But that is not the usual case. Ordinarily, in small residential work, a selected list of bidders is made up, consisting of qualified and experienced contractors. They are invited to submit a lump sum bid for which they will complete the work.

The list of bidders should consist of about five firms. Selection of contractors to make up this list may be difficult if a family is new in the community or has had no contact with the building industry.

Because the building of a home is such an important undertaking, scrutinize the contractors carefully before making a selection.

Recalling Facts

1. The author mentions the story of
   - ☐ a. the three little pigs.
   - ☐ b. Cinderella.
   - ☐ c. Sir Lancelot.

2. A person who actually builds a house is called
   - ☐ a. an architect.
   - ☐ b. an engineer.
   - ☐ c. a contractor.

3. Most building contracts are assigned as a result of
   - ☐ a. personal recommendations.
   - ☐ b. competitive bids.
   - ☐ c. previous work.

4. According to the author, building a home is
   - ☐ a. an exciting adventure.
   - ☐ b. an awesome task.
   - ☐ c. a complex operation.

5. How many bids are usually taken for a construction job?
   - ☐ a. three
   - ☐ b. five
   - ☐ c. seven

Understanding the Passage

6. Children's rhymes, stories, and songs stress the importance of
   - ☐ a. large homes.
   - ☐ b. tasteful decor.
   - ☐ c. sturdy construction.

7. In the article, the author mentions a house made of
   - ☐ a. bricks.
   - ☐ b. sticks.
   - ☐ c. stones.

8. The search for a builder is most time consuming when a
   - ☐ a. person is new to a community.
   - ☐ b. large house is to be built.
   - ☐ c. person plans to build a home in a remote area.

9. A bid usually consists of
   - ☐ a. itemized lists of construction costs.
   - ☐ b. one price for the entire job.
   - ☐ c. a cost estimate of materials only.

10. When the author mentions children's nursery stories, he is
    - ☐ a. showing the origins of certain attitudes.
    - ☐ b. discussing the history of entertainment.
    - ☐ c. implying that children are imaginative.

All natural cheese should be kept refrigerated. Soft unripened cheeses, such as cottage, cream, or Neufchatel, are perishable and should be used within a few days after purchase. Ripened or cured cheeses keep well in the refrigerator for several weeks if protected from mold contamination and drying out. The original wrapper or covering should be left on the cheese. The cut surface of cheese should be covered with wax paper, foil, or plastic wrapping material to protect the surface from drying. If large pieces are to be stored for any extended length of time, the cut surface may be dipped in hot paraffin. Small pieces may be completely rewrapped. Mold that may develop on natural cheeses is not harmful, and it is easily scraped or cut from the surface of the cheese. The particular mold in the interior of such cheeses as Blue, Gorgonzola, Roquefort, or Stilton has been carefully developed to produce the characteristic color and distinctive flavor of those varieties and is consumed as part of the cheese.

Ends or pieces of cheese that have become dried out and hard may be grated and kept refrigerated in a clean, tightly covered glass jar.

Cheese with an aromatic or strong odor such as Limburger should be stored in a tightly covered jar or container. Such cheeses are fast curing and are best when used within a reasonable time after purchase.

Normally cheese should not be allowed to freeze as this may damage the characteristic body and texture and cause the cheese to become crumbly. However, small pieces of certain varieties may be frozen satisfactorily for as long as six months if handled and stored properly. Since it is necessary that the cheese be frozen quickly, the temperature of the freezer should be zero degrees Fahrenheit or lower. Cut cheese should be carefully wrapped and then frozen immediately. Among the varieties of cheese that can be successfully frozen in small pieces are: Cheddar, Edam, Gouda, Swiss, and Provolone. Small sizes can be frozen in their original package. When removed from the freezer, cheese should be thawed in the refrigerator and used as soon as possible after thawing.

Except for soft unripened cheeses such as cottage and cream cheese, all cheese should be served unchilled in order to help bring out its distinctive flavor and texture characteristics. Cheese should be at room temperature for twenty minutes to one hour or more.

Recalling Facts

1. Unripened cheese is usually
   - ☐ a. strong tasting.
   - ☐ b. colorless.
   - ☐ c. soft textured.

2. Ripened cheeses can be kept under refrigeration for several
   - ☐ a. weeks.
   - ☐ b. months.
   - ☐ c. years.

3. Mold that forms on the surface of cheese
   - ☐ a. causes illness.
   - ☐ b. is not harmful.
   - ☐ c. is used in making paint.

4. Roquefort cheese is similar to
   - ☐ a. Edam.
   - ☐ b. Stilton.
   - ☐ c. Swiss.

5. A cheese with a strong odor is
   - ☐ a. Cheddar.
   - ☐ b. Gorgonzola.
   - ☐ c. Limburger.

Understanding the Passage

6. Neufchatel is mentioned in the article as an example of a
   - ☐ a. cheese that needs refrigeration.
   - ☐ b. popular European cheese.
   - ☐ c. cured cheese.

7. Most cheeses should be served
   - ☐ a. with fruit.
   - ☐ b. before a meal.
   - ☐ c. at room temperature.

8. The author states that great care should be taken when
   - ☐ a. buying cheese in a supermarket.
   - ☐ b. storing most cheeses with other foods.
   - ☐ c. freezing cheese.

9. The article implies that
   - ☐ a. exposure to air causes cheese to deteriorate.
   - ☐ b. only fresh milk can be used in the manufacture of cheese.
   - ☐ c. cheese that has dried out or hardened must be discarded.

10. According to the article, Blue cheese derives its color from
    - ☐ a. bacteria that is allowed to grow within the cheese.
    - ☐ b. mold that is cultured within the cheese.
    - ☐ c. the high temperatures to which the cheese is exposed.

43   Water on the Mountain

The amount of usable water has always been of great concern in parts of our West. In its early settlement, owning springs and flowing streams meant control. This control was possible without possession of large areas of grazing land. With the coming of settlers, pressure developed for possession of both water and grazing land. Disputes were common, often resulting in shoot-outs. The range war in Johnson County, Wyoming, in the 1890s is an example of armed conflict between ranchers. With the coming of statehood, laws were made to protect the water rights of settlers. Laws were made to provide an orderly procedure for the control and use of the water in the streams.

There isn't enough water in all places for everyone to use as much as he may like. Deciding on the amount that will be usable in any given period needs advance planning. This time factor allows people to manage and use available resources better. Water supply forecasts blueprint future supplies. Each major water interest needs the basic data so it can plan its operation.

Users of irrigation water adjust their use of or demand for water to the supply forecast from the winter snowpack. Reservoir levels are adjusted to either save water or release it to prevent floods. Space in a multiple-purpose reservoir can be managed better with advance information on reservoir inflow. Power companies can plan the controls that will be necessary between hydropower generation and other sources of power.

Interest is rising in the ways to increase rainfall through artificial means, such as cloud seeding. The Soil Conservation Service, under agreement with the Bureau of Reclamation, is making measurements of snow accumulation in the Park Range area near Steamboat Springs, Colorado. This is a program to determine, through research and field operations, if there is a practical way of increasing the snowfall at any time or place.

In this Colorado network of 21 snow courses, six are equipped with pressure pillows, on-site recorders, and radio telemetry. Data are sent via a repeater station to the base station at Steamboat Springs. The operator at the base station can obtain data at any time from the mountain by simply pushing a button. The entire operation is automatic. Similar work by the Soil Conservation Service is also being done in Utah and elsewhere.

Proper use of the West's water depends on advance knowledge of water on the mountain.

Recalling Facts

1. The Soil Conservation Service uses an instrument known as
   - ☐ a. a barograph.
   - ☐ b. an altimeter.
   - ☐ c. a pressure pillow.

2. The Johnson County Range War occurred in
   - ☐ a. Nevada.
   - ☐ b. Utah.
   - ☐ c. Wyoming.

3. About how many snow courses are in the Park Range?
   - ☐ a. five
   - ☐ b. ten
   - ☐ c. twenty

4. The Soil Conservation Service is studying
   - ☐ a. snow depths.
   - ☐ b. stream capacities.
   - ☐ c. methods of irrigation.

5. Steamboat Springs is located in
   - ☐ a. Colorado.
   - ☐ b. New Mexico.
   - ☐ c. Kansas.

Understanding the Passage

6. The Johnson County Range War was an example of conflict
   - ☐ a. among ranchers.
   - ☐ b. between ranchers and the federal government.
   - ☐ c. between ranchers and Indians.

7. The author implies that early settlers
   - ☐ a. built towns along riverbanks.
   - ☐ b. stole cattle from one another.
   - ☐ c. grazed animals on land they did not own.

8. Water available for irrigation in the West comes from
   - ☐ a. summer thunderstorms.
   - ☐ b. Pacific rainstorms.
   - ☐ c. winter snowstorms.

9. The author is hopeful that
   - ☐ a. hydroelectric plants can be built in many areas.
   - ☐ b. clouds can be seeded to produce rain.
   - ☐ c. drought-resistant crops can be developed.

10. Radio telemetry is used to
    - ☐ a. measure remote snow depths.
    - ☐ b. find storms before they strike land.
    - ☐ c. predict the flow of mountain streams.

In 1932, in keeping with the twentieth-century concept of honoring American Presidents on our coins, the Washington quarter was created and released to celebrate the 200th anniversary of George Washington's birth. Designed by New York sculptor John Flanagan, it carries the profile of Washington on one side and the American eagle on the other.

The eagle has been America's symbol since our country was first founded. Greece and Rome both used the eagle as a symbol on their coins as a sign of strength and faithfulness. The eagle is a magnificent bird. It is large, sometimes fierce, and always physically powerful.

Traditionally, the eagle on our American coins has signified peace and has been pictured in many different poses. Most often it is designed with its wings spread wide in a gesture of protection. Other times it is shown in flight. For the Washington quarter, designer Flanagan chose to illustrate a calm, protective eagle perched on a branch with its wings spread out.

George Washington was a man of learning, foresight, and honesty. At the age of 16, he was surveying the Shenandoah Valley. He was a colonel during the French and Indian Wars, a member of the First Continental Congress, and General of the ragged Continental Army. He was unanimously elected first President of the United States in 1789.

His military career during the French and Indian Wars was far from outstanding. In fact, twice he was responsible for serious mistakes. But later, as Commander of the Continental Army fighting during the American Revolution, his tactics were often brilliant and always successful. If he had not kept his army at work for six years, the Revolution would certainly have failed.

After the war, he planned to retire to Mount Vernon and return to plantation life. Instead he was persuaded to preside over the Constitutional Convention of 1787, where the delegates decided he should be the first President. Washington, on the other hand, was afraid that people would lower their opinion of him if he became President.

On the day of his inauguration, he stood before the assembly in humility and pride, but he was so nervous that at times he could scarcely be heard in the room. He apologized to the Congress for being a person who had inherited "inferior endowments from nature and was unpracticed in the duties of civil administration." He served two successive terms with high distinction.

Recalling Facts

1. The Washington quarter was released during the early
   - ☐ a. 1920s.
   - ☐ b. 1930s.
   - ☐ c. 1940s.

2. The sculptor who designed the Washington quarter was from
   - ☐ a. France.
   - ☐ b. Greece.
   - ☐ c. New York.

3. Traditionally, the eagle on the United States coins has symbolized
   - ☐ a. peace.
   - ☐ b. courage.
   - ☐ c. victory.

4. What country once used the eagle on its coins?
   - ☐ a. France
   - ☐ b. Greece
   - ☐ c. Germany

5. At the age of 16, Washington was a
   - ☐ a. colonel.
   - ☐ b. tax assessor.
   - ☐ c. surveyor.

Understanding the Passage

6. Washington probably looked upon the French and Indian Wars as
   - ☐ a. a tragic defeat.
   - ☐ b. an unimportant conflict.
   - ☐ c. a learning experience.

7. According to the author, Washington's army
   - ☐ a. showed remarkable endurance.
   - ☐ b. was poorly equipped.
   - ☐ c. suffered terribly during winter months.

8. Washington accepted the Presidency with
   - ☐ a. some reluctance.
   - ☐ b. great enthusiasm.
   - ☐ c. surprising bitterness.

9. The author implies that the eagle on the Washington quarter
   - ☐ a. represents the leadership of Washington.
   - ☐ b. signifies the birth of a new nation.
   - ☐ c. symbolizes the unity of the first colonies.

10. In the middle of the article, the author changes the topic to the
   - ☐ a. importance of birds on United States coins.
   - ☐ b. life of George Washington.
   - ☐ c. history of the Washington quarter.

45 Setting Up Shop

The key to starting a new business in the plastics industry is to create a product that can be produced and sold and to establish the technical ability to produce it. In some cases, the individual who enters the plastics business may, through his knowledge of another industry, have discovered how a new item can be made in plastics. He may be able to establish the existence of a market for his business. His next step is to make sure that he can arrange to find the necessary technical ability to produce efficiently and economically.

The person proposing to start such a new business should have some ideas about what he wants to produce and where he can sell it. These ideas should stem from his own experience. It is unlikely that someone can enter the plastics business without previous background in the industry and establish a product line by trial and error afterwards. Moreover, no one would advance money on such a basis.

The starting point, therefore, would be an individual or a group of individuals who have some ideas, based on their own experience, about what they want to produce and to whom they propose to sell their product. The next step is to verify this market. A market survey should be made.

If the product is a new line, samples will be required and visits will have to be made to future customers to determine their reaction to the line and the price at which it can be sold. Prospective customers can give the market surveyor an idea of how many of the items they might expect to purchase at a given price.

If the proposed new business is to provide a variety of products to an existing industry, the market surveyor should canvass proposed accounts within the industry to develop some estimates of the total volume of business, its growth pattern, the competition, and the pricing arrangements. Here again, the information can be used to develop estimates of volume and revenues.

If the individuals proposing to start the new business do not have the technical ability, they should next arrange to acquire a production supervisor. An advertisement in the trade press might secure inquiries from someone who is presently a production supervisor or an assistant. To offer a partnership to such a person, particularly if he is well experienced, will be a key to success in the business.

Recalling Facts

1. It is unlikely that someone
   can enter the plastics
   business without
   □ a. capital.
   □ b. a license.
   □ c. prior experience.

2. A product line in plastics
   should be established through
   □ a. careful planning.
   □ b. trial and error.
   □ c. purposeful reading.

3. To verify a potential market, a
   person should
   □ a. advertise.
   □ b. take a survey.
   □ c. offer gifts.

4. Prices are established
   in part by
   □ a. prospective customers.
   □ b. production supervisors.
   □ c. federal regulations.

5. An assistant can be recruited
   through the
   □ a. employment agency.
   □ b. local newspaper.
   □ c. trade press.

Understanding the Passage

6. The author offers information on
   □ a. small businesses that
        have succeeded.
   □ b. starting a small business.
   □ c. production techniques.

7. A production supervisor
   □ a. works closely with the
        personnel office.
   □ b. is the first person who should
        be hired in the new firm.
   □ c. can share the responsibilities
        and profits of the company.

8. The information presented
   suggests that
   □ a. a business can be
        established from scratch.
   □ b. most businesses depend on the
        Small Business Administration.
   □ c. many small businesses go
        bankrupt within a year.

9. The author points out that a
   person without technical ability
   □ a. should never think of
        starting a business.
   □ b. can seek out experienced
        individuals for help.
   □ c. can still do well by manu-
        facturing on a small scale.

10. It can be concluded that
    □ a. the government is always will-
         ing to help new businessmen.
    □ b. a variety of products can be
         produced in one plastics plant.
    □ c. new product lines are
         difficult to advertise.

The Milwaukee County Zoo, where bars on cages are virtually eliminated and animals live in their own natural, open environment, is a sort of zoo paradise. The Milwaukee Zoo has been a leader in the new wave of zoo construction, emphasizing natural habitat.

The concept is not only psychologically healthy for animals but educational for visitors as well. People unconsciously respect animals when they see them in their natural state.

Imagine antelopes, zebras, pelicans, and ostriches roaming about their outdoor sanctuary, seemingly within striking distance of their natural enemy, the lion.

But the prey are not concerned. They're safe because a dry moat 22 feet wide and 15 feet deep has been dug. Lions can't possibly leap it, and humans just don't notice it. In some cases, the moat is the only separation between the sidewalk and a group of carnivores.

One exception to the total environment theme is the leopard, much too agile to live peacefully with the moat. In this case, thin safety glass is used, but never bars. The glass has worked well. It's easily cleaned, pleasant for its residents, and permits almost the same natural feeling as the outdoor areas.

Another unusual aspect of the zoo is its policy of changing its residents' environment. Periodically the beasts are shifted to give them a new neighbor, a slightly different view, or a new piece of equipment.

The Milwaukee Zoo has also perfected some landscaping innovations with its huge boulders, hills, and rocks. Actually, what appear to be natural solid granite formations throughout the zoo are entirely man-made from simulated granite. For each rock group in the zoo, a quarter-inch scale model was built. Every crevice and angle was hand built with steel framework; papered, cemented, and finally sculpted for realism.

One of the largest in the United States, the Milwaukee Zoo covers 184 lush acres. It's easy to tour because of its convenient arrangement. All of the buildings, such as the monkey house, reptile house, aquarium, and small mammal house, are located in the same general vicinity, which is tucked away in the trees. The aviary, known as one of the finest in the world because it so accurately depicts the birds' natural habitat, is the first exhibit beyond the main entry.

The largest portion of the site is devoted to the geographical groupings easily accessible by sidewalks and color coded on the visitor's zoo map.

Reading Time _____   *Comprehension Score* _____   *Words per Minute* _____   105

Recalling Facts

1. The Milwaukee County Zoo features
   - ☐ a. rare animals.
   - ☐ b. natural habitat.
   - ☐ c. modern architecture.

2. Lions are separated from other animals by a
   - ☐ a. canal.
   - ☐ b. moat.
   - ☐ c. fence.

3. A visitor to the Milwaukee County Zoo would never find
   - ☐ a. bars.
   - ☐ b. glass enclosures.
   - ☐ c. wild animals.

4. The granite formations in the zoo are
   - ☐ a. African imports.
   - ☐ b. native to the area.
   - ☐ c. man-made.

5. The size of the Milwaukee Zoo is nearly
   - ☐ a. 50 acres.
   - ☐ b. 100 acres.
   - ☐ c. 200 acres.

Understanding the Passage

6. The author implies that lions
   - ☐ a. eat their food after visitors have left.
   - ☐ b. live longer than most wild animals.
   - ☐ c. cannot leap as far as leopards can.

7. The leopard is not as free as other animals because it is
   - ☐ a. the most dangerous animal in the zoo.
   - ☐ b. able to leap great distances.
   - ☐ c. unable to live peacefully with larger animals.

8. The zoo's policy of changing the location of its animals
   - ☐ a. indicates that animals may become bored.
   - ☐ b. shows that management is experimenting with cage sizes.
   - ☐ c. proves that animals destroy their surroundings.

9. The aviary at the zoo is
   - ☐ a. the most popular attraction.
   - ☐ b. often the visitor's last stop.
   - ☐ c. noted for its realism.

10. We can conclude that the Milwaukee Zoo is
    - ☐ a. innovative.
    - ☐ b. expensive to visit.
    - ☐ c. financed by local businesses.

47 The Magic Potion Notion

Drug abuse is like a communicable disease. It spreads by example, by word of mouth, and by imitation. Drug abuse is certainly increasing, but so is the number of young people who have tried drugs and want to stay away from them. As we provide treatment services for them, these young people become able to tell other youth that the drug scene is not as great as they thought is was before they became addicted. And, of greater importance, the experiences of these young people are believed by their peers before experimentation becomes a habit.

Parents can help prevent drug usage by their example, by their knowledge, and by their understanding. If they desire to talk to their children about drugs, they must be informed. Usually they know far less about drugs than their children do. Ideally, before their child is tempted to experiment, they will have been able to explain to him the futility of the life dependent upon drugs and, even more convincing to young people, the actual damage that a drug abuser does to his body.

Parents may panic when they find evidence that their child is using drugs. But this emotion, though understandable, is not likely to help. Drug experimentation does not necessarily mean that a youth has a psychological problem and needs help. Most adolescent drug abusers are not regular users. Nor are their parents necessarily to blame for their experimenting with drugs, since pressure from their peers is far more convincing to many young people than advice from parents.

While parents have a duty to speak loudly and convincingly on the subject if drug abuse occurs, their greatest influence will come from the example they set. If they use legal drugs to excess and dole them out unthinkingly, they are training their children to view "pill popping" as normal. If they use alcohol as a crutch, they will have a difficult time in persuading sons or daughters to desist from alcohol or drug usage.

While the parents' action is legal and their children's action is not, they are setting examples of escapism that will probably be imitated. As adults, parents have the opportunity to discourage, by their own example and not merely by words, the "magic potion notion" that drugs can be the remedy for all ills and that a random sampling or overuse of chemicals will bring instant happiness or relief from problems.

Recalling Facts

1. The author compares drug abuse with
   - ☐ a. alcoholism.
   - ☐ b. mental illness.
   - ☐ c. communicable disease.

2. The author states that "pill popping" is a form of
   - ☐ a. exhibitionism.
   - ☐ b. escapism.
   - ☐ c. activism.

3. Young people are often dissuaded from using drugs because of
   - ☐ a. school programs.
   - ☐ b. legal problems.
   - ☐ c. fear of damage.

4. Parents can help prevent their children from using drugs by
   - ☐ a. setting a good example.
   - ☐ b. following a strict code of discipline.
   - ☐ c. giving teenagers freedom without responsibility.

5. When a parent finds evidence that his child is using drugs, he often
   - ☐ a. seeks help.
   - ☐ b. panics.
   - ☐ c. calls the police.

Understanding the Passage

6. The author states that
   - ☐ a. parents know less than their children about drugs.
   - ☐ b. drug use is decreasing.
   - ☐ c. some people become addicted to drugs because of insecurity.

7. According to the author, young people experiment with drugs because
   - ☐ a. they are unable to communicate with their parents.
   - ☐ b. their parents are too restrictive.
   - ☐ c. they are unable to resist peer pressures.

8. The drug scene is showing signs of change as more and more young people are
   - ☐ a. becoming addicted to hard drugs.
   - ☐ b. turning to religion for fulfillment.
   - ☐ c. seeking help in breaking the drug habit.

9. Most adolescent drug abusers
   - ☐ a. learn about drugs from relatives.
   - ☐ b. eventually become addicted.
   - ☐ c. are involved in experimentation.

10. The "magic potion notion" refers to
    - ☐ a. taking drugs to achieve instant happiness.
    - ☐ b. finding a universal cure for drug addiction.
    - ☐ c. solving drug problems through government controls.

Never before have so many cosmetics been available to make men and women more attractive, more desirable, and more socially acceptable. Never before have Americans used such a wide variety and large volume of cosmetic products.

Most of these products are safe for use, but it is very important that some commonsense safety rules are observed. The Food and Drug Administration is the federal agency that has been assigned by the Congress to assure the safety of the American cosmetics supply. The Federal Food, Drug, and Cosmetic Act defines a cosmetic as an article that is to be rubbed, poured, sprinkled, or sprayed onto the body to cleanse, beautify, promote attractiveness, or change appearance.

The law gives the FDA authority to take legal action against a cosmetic only after its dangers can be proved in a court of law. The FDA does not have the authority to review the safety of cosmetics or their ingredients before they are sold to the public.

To fulfill its duty under the law, the FDA constantly tests cosmetic products for unsafe substances or harmful bacteria. The priority for this testing is based on consumer complaints about specific cosmetic products. Whenever a trend seems to be developing in consumer complaints, the FDA gives its attention to the group of cosmetics causing these complaints.

Among the types of products that cause most complaints are deodorants and antiperspirants, hair preparations, and makeup for the eyes. Often the adverse effect, reported by the consumer, is not serious and disappears when use of the particular product is discontinued. But improper use of some cosmetics can cause serious and permanent injury.

In the past few years, the cosmetics industry has come a long way in providing further guarantees that cosmetics are safe and properly labeled. Cosmetics companies test their products for safety in various laboratories.

Recently, the cosmetics industry trade association, the Cosmetic, Toiletry, and Fragrance Association (CTFA), developed with the FDA a voluntary program that should assist the FDA's efforts in assuring that cosmetics are harmless. The first step of the program is the voluntary listing of cosmetic firms with the FDA. The second step calls for the manufacturers to list with the FDA the ingredients in their products, except for flavors and fragrances. The third step requires companies to provide the FDA with information on all consumer complaints they receive.

These programs should contribute toward even greater assurances that cosmetics will be safe.

Recalling Facts

1. The agency responsible for regulating the safety of cosmetics is the
   - ☐ a. Cosmetics Bureau.
   - ☐ b. International Cosmetics Council.
   - ☐ c. Food and Drug Administration.

2. A cosmetic is not expected to
   - ☐ a. cleanse.
   - ☐ b. beautify.
   - ☐ c. nourish.

3. For action to be taken against a cosmetic, it must be proven harmful in
   - ☐ a. an opinion poll.
   - ☐ b. a court of law.
   - ☐ c. research laboratories.

4. Cosmetics are tested constantly for
   - ☐ a. discoloration.
   - ☐ b. bacteria.
   - ☐ c. texture.

5. Among the types of products that cause complaints are
   - ☐ a. deodorants.
   - ☐ b. face creams.
   - ☐ c. nail polishes.

Understanding the Passage

6. The author points out that cosmetics generally
   - ☐ a. are now more popular than ever before.
   - ☐ b. have changed little over the years.
   - ☐ c. cause serious and permanent illnesses.

7. Some cosmetics firms
   - ☐ a. are now manufacturing all-natural cosmetics.
   - ☐ b. guarantee that their products are safe.
   - ☐ c. refuse to answer customer complaints.

8. The first step in the CTFA program assuring cosmetics safety is
   - ☐ a. listing ingredients in products.
   - ☐ b. providing information on all consumer complaints.
   - ☐ c. registering with the federal regulatory agency.

9. The author implies that
   - ☐ a. the government is lenient with cosmetics firms.
   - ☐ b. customer complaints carry some weight.
   - ☐ c. foreign cosmetics are more popular than domestic brands.

10. We can conclude that
    - ☐ a. cosmetics are a billion-dollar-a-year business.
    - ☐ b. tighter controls are being placed on the cosmetics industry.
    - ☐ c. cosmetics firms do not cooperate with government agencies.

49 Fifteen Tons a Minute

New York City is accustomed to being first, largest, or best known in a lot of things. It accepts innovation as commonplace, a part of daily life. But one of its innovations stands out as truly remarkable, even to New Yorkers.

On May 17, 1967, dignitaries and well-wishers from all over the world gathered at Hunts Point in the Bronx to witness the dedication of the largest and most modern wholesale produce market ever constructed. The market stands on 126 acres of land with buildings that would stretch almost 1½ miles if placed end to end, and cost $38 million to build. This became home for almost an entire industry that had moved from its former location in lower Manhattan, twelve miles away.

Presidential representatives and other federal, state, local, and industrial officials heard New York City's mayor describe the new fruit and vegetable market as just the beginning of a giant wholesale food distribution center. Final plans called for filling 350 acres of land with facilities to handle all kinds of food for millions of people in the New York City area.

What New York's mayor called "just the beginning" for his metropolis would have already been an avalanche for most other cities. Nearly fifteen tons of fresh produce come here each minute of every daylight hour of every working day. About one in every eight carloads of fresh fruits and vegetables produced in the United States for sale in unprocessed form finds its way to this market where it joins with products from 35 foreign countries to be distributed to consumers.

This market handles produce from nearly every state, as well as practically every kind of commercial produce grown in the world.

The individuality of this market did not come with the building of this new facility. This is something the New York wholesalers already had earned through generations of hard work. Authorities believe it all started near the piers at the southernmost tip of Manhattan, for here is where ships brought goods to early New Yorkers. A large part of the food arrived at these piers, and the original food handlers located near the place where it was unloaded.

For reasons known only to them, the food wholesalers gradually moved north to an area along Washington Street. They settled into any kind of housing that was available and worked for over 100 years while the country's largest metropolis grew around them.

Recalling Facts

1. The new produce market was built in
   - ☐ a. Brooklyn.
   - ☐ b. Queens.
   - ☐ c. the Bronx.

2. The construction of the market cost more than
   - ☐ a. $35 million.
   - ☐ b. $50 million.
   - ☐ c. $65 million.

3. Authorities believe that the first produce market was located
   - ☐ a. on Staten Island.
   - ☐ b. in Manhattan.
   - ☐ c. in Queens.

4. The old market was in operation for about
   - ☐ a. 50 years.
   - ☐ b. 75 years.
   - ☐ c. 100 years.

5. Ultimately, the produce facility will cover
   - ☐ a. 126 acres.
   - ☐ b. 225 acres.
   - ☐ c. 350 acres.

Understanding the Passage

6. A new market was built because
   - ☐ a. of zoning regulations.
   - ☐ b. more room and better facilities were needed.
   - ☐ c. the old market burned down.

7. The title of the article, "Fifteen Tons a Minute," refers to the
   - ☐ a. amount of produce arriving at the market.
   - ☐ b. rate at which the new structure was built.
   - ☐ c. amount of food unloaded from ships each day.

8. At the new market, a visitor would not find
   - ☐ a. household shoppers.
   - ☐ b. imported goods.
   - ☐ c. wholesale buyers.

9. Washington Street was famous for many years as the site of
   - ☐ a. slaughter houses.
   - ☐ b. quaint shops.
   - ☐ c. food markets.

10. We can conclude that
    - ☐ a. the United States is the world's largest exporter of grain.
    - ☐ b. New York City has the largest marketplace in the country.
    - ☐ c. the opening of the new market was a commonplace event to New Yorkers.

50 Curds and Whey

Many countries have developed one or more varieties of cheese peculiar to their own conditions and culture.

When the colonists settled in the New World, they brought with them their own methods of making their favorite kinds of cheese. The first cheddar cheese factory in the United States was built by Jesse Williams in Rome, Oneida County, New York, in 1851. As the population increased in the East and there was a corresponding increase in the demand for market milk, the cheese industry gradually moved westward. Cheesemaking in the United States and in the other leading cheese-producing countries of the world is now largely a factory industry.

Many of the popular varieties, although originating in Europe, are now produced in the United States and are available in most food stores, delicatessens, and specialty cheese stores.

The making of natural cheese is an art centuries old. It consists of separating most of the mild solids from the milk by curdling with rennet or bacterial culture or both, and then separating the curd from the whey by heating, stirring, and pressing. Most cheeses in this country are made from whole milk. For certain types of cheeses both milk and cream are used. For other types, skim milk, whey, or mixtures of all of these are used.

The distinctive flavor, body, and texture characteristics of the various cheeses are the results of the kind of milk used; the method used for curdling the milk and for cutting, cooking, and forming the curd; the type of bacteria or molds used in ripening; the amount of salt or other seasonings added and the conditions of ripening such as temperature, humidity, and length of time. Sometimes only minor differences in the procedures followed may make the difference between one variety of cheese and another.

After the cheese has been formed into its characteristic shape, it is given a coating of wax or other protective coating or wrapping. It is then allowed to cure or age for varying lengths of time, depending upon the kind or variety of cheese being made.

When the cheese has reached its proper curing stage, it is often cut or sliced from larger blocks or wheels into more suitable sizes for consumer use. The refrigerated showcase in a modern food market is most enticing with its display of various sizes of cheese packages in such shapes as wedges, oblongs, cubes, slices, and blocks.

Recalling Facts

1. The first cheddar cheese factory in the United States was built in
   - ☐ a. Maryland.
   - ☐ b. New York.
   - ☐ c. Virginia.

2. According to the article, rennet is used to
   - ☐ a. curdle milk.
   - ☐ b. sour milk.
   - ☐ c. produce bacteria.

3. Most cheeses in this country are made from
   - ☐ a. cream.
   - ☐ b. skim milk.
   - ☐ c. whole milk.

4. What ingredient is added to most cheeses?
   - ☐ a. salt
   - ☐ b. yeast
   - ☐ c. monosodium glutamate

5. The first cheddar cheese factory in the United States was built during the middle
   - ☐ a. 1600s.
   - ☐ b. 1700s.
   - ☐ c. 1800s.

Understanding the Passage

6. This article is mostly about
   - ☐ a. manufacturing cheese.
   - ☐ b. buying and storing cheese.
   - ☐ c. importing cheeses from Europe.

7. The article implies that
   - ☐ a. most people do not like strong cheeses.
   - ☐ b. the United States is one of the largest cheese-producing countries.
   - ☐ c. Wisconsin produces more cheese than any other state.

8. The cheese industry moved westward as the
   - ☐ a. need for cheaper labor became apparent.
   - ☐ b. raising of cattle became more common in the West.
   - ☐ c. demand for milk increased in the East.

9. The reader can infer that whey is
   - ☐ a. thin and watery.
   - ☐ b. thick and creamy.
   - ☐ c. thick and lumpy.

10. We can conclude from this article that
    - ☐ a. many factors influence the flavor of cheese.
    - ☐ b. cheese is very high in protein.
    - ☐ c. cheddar cheese originated in America.

Answer Key

Progress Graph

Pacing Graph

Answer Key

1	1. b	2. c	3. c	4. c	5. b	6. b	7. b	8. c	9. c	10. a
2	1. c	2. a	3. c	4. c	5. c	6. a	7. b	8. c	9. a	10. a
3	1. a	2. a	3. c	4. b	5. c	6. c	7. c	8. b	9. c	10. a
4	1. c	2. b	3. b	4. b	5. c	6. a	7. c	8. a	9. b	10. a
5	1. c	2. c	3. a	4. c	5. b	6. c	7. c	8. c	9. b	10. b
6	1. a	2. b	3. b	4. a	5. c	6. a	7. c	8. a	9. a	10. b
7	1. c	2. c	3. a	4. b	5. c	6. c	7. a	8. c	9. b	10. a
8	1. a	2. c	3. c	4. b	5. c	6. c	7. a	8. a	9. b	10. b
9	1. a	2. c	3. b	4. a	5. c	6. c	7. b	8. c	9. a	10. a
10	1. b	2. a	3. b	4. c	5. a	6. a	7. b	8. c	9. a	10. a
11	1. c	2. c	3. c	4. a	5. b	6. b	7. b	8. c	9. c	10. b
12	1. c	2. a	3. b	4. a	5. b	6. a	7. c	8. b	9. c	10. a
13	1. a	2. b	3. b	4. b	5. a	6. a	7. b	8. b	9. b	10. a
14	1. c	2. c	3. a	4. c	5. c	6. a	7. c	8. c	9. a	10. b
15	1. a	2. c	3. c	4. c	5. b	6. c	7. b	8. a	9. c	10. a
16	1. a	2. c	3. a	4. c	5. b	6. c	7. c	8. a	9. b	10. b
17	1. a	2. b	3. a	4. c	5. b	6. a	7. c	8. a	9. c	10. a
18	1. b	2. c	3. a	4. a	5. a	6. a	7. c	8. c	9. b	10. b
19	1. c	2. a	3. a	4. b	5. a	6. b	7. c	8. a	9. c	10. a
20	1. b	2. a	3. a	4. c	5. a	6. c	7. c	8. b	9. b	10. c
21	1. c	2. b	3. c	4. a	5. a	6. b	7. a	8. c	9. b	10. a
22	1. c	2. b	3. b	4. c	5. b	6. a	7. b	8. a	9. a	10. a
23	1. c	2. b	3. a	4. c	5. b	6. c	7. b	8. c	9. a	10. a
24	1. c	2. a	3. a	4. c	5. b	6. a	7. b	8. c	9. b	10. a
25	1. a	2. b	3. c	4. b	5. a	6. b	7. b	8. b	9. c	10. a

26	1. c	2. b	3. a	4. b	5. b	6. b	7. b	8. c	9. a	10. a
27	1. a	2. a	3. c	4. c	5. c	6. c	7. b	8. c	9. c	10. a
28	1. b	2. a	3. b	4. c	5. b	6. a	7. c	8. b	9. c	10. a
29	1. b	2. a	3. c	4. b	5. a	6. b	7. a	8. c	9. a	10. b
30	1. c	2. a	3. b	4. a	5. c	6. a	7. b	8. a	9. b	10. a
31	1. b	2. c	3. b	4. a	5. a	6. c	7. c	8. a	9. b	10. c
32	1. c	2. b	3. b	4. b	5. b	6. a	7. c	8. a	9. b	10. a
33	1. a	2. c	3. a	4. b	5. c	6. a	7. a	8. c	9. a	10. b
34	1. c	2. a	3. c	4. a	5. c	6. a	7. c	8. b	9. a	10. a
35	1. c	2. a	3. c	4. a	5. a	6. c	7. b	8. c	9. c	10. a
36	1. a	2. a	3. a	4. a	5. b	6. a	7. c	8. c	9. a	10. b
37	1. c	2. b	3. b	4. c	5. b	6. b	7. c	8. c	9. a	10. a
38	1. a	2. c	3. c	4. a	5. c	6. b	7. a	8. c	9. b	10. c
39	1. c	2. c	3. b	4. b	5. a	6. c	7. c	8. b	9. b	10. a
40	1. a	2. b	3. c	4. a	5. c	6. b	7. b	8. a	9. b	10. a
41	1. a	2. c	3. b	4. b	5. b	6. c	7. b	8. a	9. b	10. a
42	1. c	2. a	3. b	4. b	5. c	6. a	7. c	8. c	9. a	10. b
43	1. c	2. c	3. c	4. a	5. a	6. a	7. c	8. c	9. b	10. a
44	1. b	2. c	3. a	4. b	5. c	6. c	7. a	8. a	9. a	10. b
45	1. c	2. a	3. b	4. a	5. c	6. b	7. c	8. a	9. b	10. b
46	1. b	2. b	3. a	4. c	5. c	6. c	7. b	8. a	9. c	10. a
47	1. c	2. b	3. c	4. a	5. b	6. a	7. c	8. c	9. c	10. a
48	1. c	2. c	3. b	4. b	5. a	6. a	7. b	8. c	9. b	10. b
49	1. c	2. a	3. b	4. c	5. c	6. b	7. a	8. a	9. c	10. b
50	1. b	2. a	3. c	4. a	5. c	6. a	7. b	8. c	9. a	10. a

Progress Graph (1–25)

Directions: Write your comprehension score in the box under the selection number. Then put an x on the line above each box to show your reading time and words-per-minute reading rate.

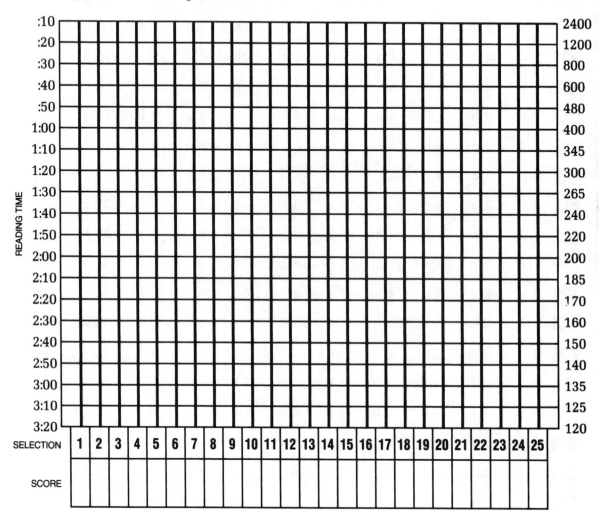

READING TIME		WPM
:10		2400
:20		1200
:30		800
:40		600
:50		480
1:00		400
1:10		345
1:20		300
1:30		265
1:40		240
1:50		220
2:00		200
2:10		185
2:20		170
2:30		160
2:40		150
2:50		140
3:00		135
3:10		125
3:20		120

SELECTION: 1 2 3 4 5 6 7 8 9 10 11 12 13 14 15 16 17 18 19 20 21 22 23 24 25

SCORE

Progress Graph (26–50)

Directions: Write your comprehension score in the box under the selection number. Then put an x on the line above each box to show your reading time and words-per-minute reading rate.

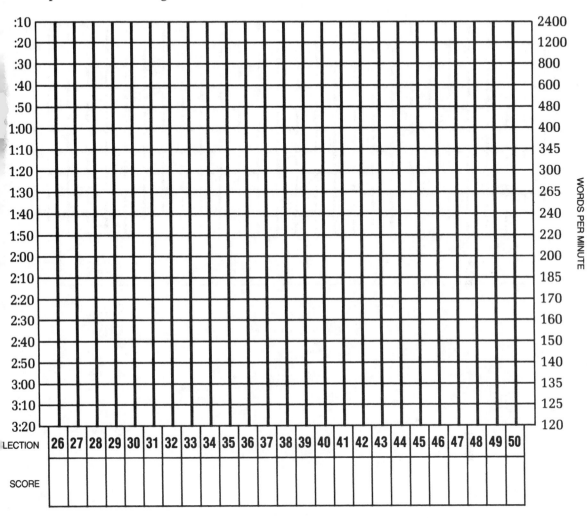

:10																								2400
:20																								1200
:30																								800
:40																								600
:50																								480
1:00																								400
1:10																								345
1:20																								300
1:30																								265
1:40																								240
1:50																								220
2:00																								200
2:10																								185
2:20																								170
2:30																								160
2:40																								150
2:50																								140
3:00																								135
3:10																								125
3:20																								120

WORDS PER MINUTE

SELECTION	26	27	28	29	30	31	32	33	34	35	36	37	38	39	40	41	42	43	44	45	46	47	48	49	50
SCORE																									

Pacing Graph

Directions: In the boxes labeled "Pace" along the bottom of the graph, write your words-per-minute rate. On the vertical line above each box, put an x to indicate your comprehension score.

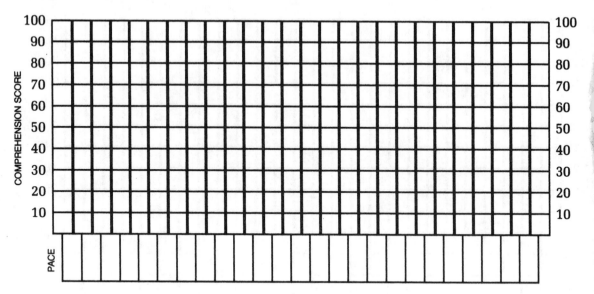